THE BAHAMAS

George Hunte

THE BAHAMAS

B. T. Batsford Ltd
London & Sydney

The Author and Publishers would like to thank the following for permission to use photographs in this book : the Bahamas Ministry of Tourism; the Bahamas Tourist News Bureau and Frederic Maura, Wendell Cleare; the Cotton Bay Club; Infoplan, Frankfurt; the Mansell Collection; the National Maritime Museum; the National Portrait Gallery.

First published 1975
© George Hunte 1975

Printed by Bristol Typesetting Co Ltd,
Barton Manor, St Philips Bristol
for the publishers B. T. Batsford Ltd of
4 Fitzhardinge Street, London W1H 0AH
and 23 Cross Street, Brookvale, N.S.W. 2100,
Australia

ISBN 0 7134 2992 5

Contents

Acknowledgments

Most of my approaches to the Bahamas have been made in planes of BOAC (British Airways), and from these individual experiences am happy to report that there is no exaggeration in the claim that BOAC takes good care of you. I owe a special debt of gratitude to Richard Hilary, former Commercial Director of BOAC, and Robert H. Cook, District Sales Manager in Nassau, for friendly assistance in getting material for this book. From Som Chib, Dann Lewis, Bob Duffet, Jim Southon, Joseph Delaney, Joe Edwards, Eric Wilmot, Edward Ellis and other representatives of the Ministry of Tourism I obtained superlative co-operation and by Jesse Boynton, Mrs Purcell Hepburn and other officials of Bahamasair I was given every facility at a time when the airline was still involved in reorganization.

Mrs Page Arey of the Bahama Out Island Association and Miss Mo Morris of Morris Associates in London were particularly helpful in arranging the specific visit I made to the islands in 1973. They smoothed the way and made it possible for me to obtain a great deal of updated information from experts on many islands. So many people in the Bahamas have been helpful that I cannot find space to thank them all. Among them however I must make special mention of George Meyers, General Manager of the Nassau Beach Hotel, Mr and Mrs Franz Gross of the Cotton Bay Club, Hans Zaunmayr of Treasure Cay Beach Hotel, Tom Siegel of Club Peace and Plenty, Mr and Mrs Richard Rogers of Pretty Molly Bay Club, Rawle Maynard of George Town, Roy and Mrs Schmidt of Romora Bay Club, Netica Symonette of Cape Eleuthera Villas, Brian Little of the British Land Resources Division, Dr Gay of Nassau, Major Bernard of Freeport, Don and Judy Dawes of the Lofty Fig, Marsh Harbour, J. B. Barry of North Eleuthera, Roger Westoby of the Halcyon Balmoral Hotel and Peter Kushka of Stella Maris Inn.

I have also to acknowledge courtesies received from the British High Commissioner in Nassau, the Bahamian High Commissioner to the United Kingdom and members of their staff. I am especially grateful to Mike Lonsdale for making it easy for me to obtain information from a number of people to whom I also express my thanks.

Finally I would like to thank the Minister of Tourism, Mr Clement Maynard for giving up so much time to tell me of his hopes and plans for the Bahamas, and Mr William Kalis for making the appointment.

Once again I am indebted to my wife Emma for her cheerful readiness to type this manuscript.

Illustrations

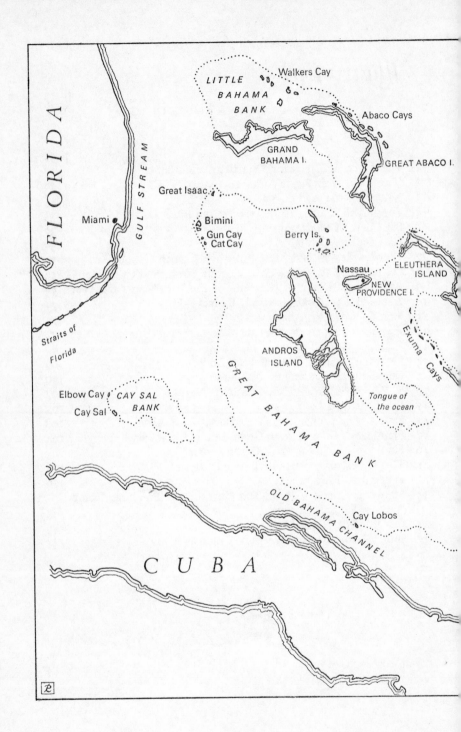

THE BAHAMA ISLANDS

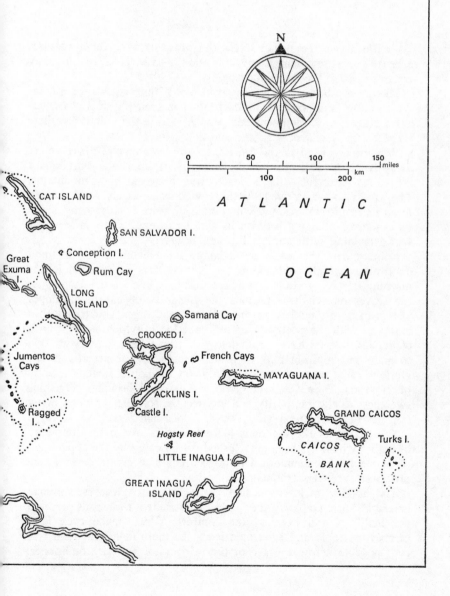

N

| 0 | 50 | 100 | 150 miles |

100   200 km

A T L A N T I C

CAT ISLAND

SAN SALVADOR I.

Conception I.

Great Exuma I.

Rum Cay

O C E A N

LONG ISLAND

Samaná Cay

CROOKED I.

French Cays

Jumentos Cays

MAYAGUANA I.

ACKLINS I.

Castle I.

Ragged I.

Hogsty Reef

GRAND CAICOS

LITTLE INAGUA I.

Turks I.

CAICOS

BANK

GREAT INAGUA ISLAND

Introduction

To write about the Bahamas for the prospective traveller requires a broad-brush treatment if any indication is to be given of the many options open to the discriminating.

There are so many choices available within dozens of islands which differ enormously from each other in their physical characteristics, stages of development and people. Within these divisions there is great variety of places to stay and things to do.

Wherever you go in the Bahamas however you will never be far away from the sea. The islands are no place for those yearning for escape to peaceful villages landlocked between high mountains. They exist to be enjoyed by those who passionately love the sea in all its manifestations and who obtain pleasure from moving above its bosom or plunging beneath its surface to explore an underwater world teeming with strange life and beauty.

Contact with the sea in the Bahamas immediately brings to mind expressions which go back to the earliest days of creation in the morning of the world. Everywhere within sound of the lapping of the waves on windswept sands the freshness of nature envelopes you with a soft tenderness that caresses and urges you to relax in harmony with the poetry of natural creation in which fish and birds plants and flowers have a full share. The sun which roasts your skin to many shades from pink to golden brown helps especially in the glorious early morning or late afternoon to induce further feelings of euphoria. Even the rain comes as a friend bringing refreshing sweetness to cleanse, purify and moisten the soil that provides many textures of green upon grass, vines, fronds and leaves.

The beauty of the islands is to be found mainly in the simplicity of nature which has been embellished considerably by the application of men who have smoothed its ragged edges to create oases where previously wildness triumphed.

The holiday maker will find peace in plenty wherever human enterprise has prepared the paths, constructed the roads, erected the buildings and installed the comforts which make even brief escapes to tropic and sub-tropic lands far more delightful than was ever possible before the age of the refrigerator and air conditioner.

All that the visitor to the Bahamas requires today, apart from the money to pay, is to know in advance the type of island holiday he is seeking, the means he wants to employ to get there and the places in which he wants to sleep while there. So many choices are open that it would be possible to spend several months at sea moving from island to island on voyages of discovery, in fishing or investigating the wonders of the reefs, caves or blue holes. Or further dimensions may be gained by combined journeys by air, sea and land which collectively could be acquired over many years.

Ordinarily, however, the majority of visitors to the Bahamas go there for periods of a few days or weeks to enjoy holidays which have been carefully "packaged" for them in advance by tour operators or travel agents who have acquired special insights into the habits of their clients.

I make no pretension in this book to have produced an "open sesame" which will at once persuade the reader that the Bahamian holiday he seeks is to be found on any particular island. All that I have been able to do on several visits to the islands extending over a period from 1945 to 1973 is to record something as I see it of an infinite variety which too seldom occurs in normal conversation when the word "Bahamas" has been pronounced. Far too many ordinary people, inclusive of some image persuaders, are quite content to dismiss the Bahamas as Nassau, Freeport and spits of sand. These three entities are of course to be found within the Bahamas but there is so much more besides. There is for example the remarkable friendliness of the Bahamian people with whom the visitor comes in contact. I found this everywhere, even in Nassau and Freeport, which are the most highly developed and the most sophisticated cities of the archipelago. Whatever forces went to shape the character of the relatively small number of people who live in the Bahamas today the dominant trait of the Bahamian is to be found in recognition of a common humanity beween peoples. Problems galore exist within the fabric of Bahamian society and are apparently being tackled in accordance with the wishes of most Bahamians, but Bahamian problems are consequences of a past which has disappeared into the corridors of history.

It is the quality of today's Bahamian people on which the future rests. I can only record that nowhere on any of the islands which I visited did I meet anyone who has caused me to change my confirmed view that there is a confidence about the Bahamian people in their ability to shape their future destiny far more genuine than I have found elsewhere in the Caribbean except in Trinidad.

Closeness to mainland territories in both cases may be possible explanations or contact with a variety of civilisations. What matters however is that the Bahamian has developed a willingness to face situations which arise unexpectedly, as for a sailor at sea. The seas around them, the distances which separate them, will perhaps in the last analysis be seen as the most formative influence upon a diversity of people whose history as a nation is only in its infancy. Who will not wish them well?

For Alison and Marion

" When the plantation grows to strength, then it is time to plant with women as well as with men; that the plantation may spread unto generations."

Francis Bacon. Essay on plantations

I BACKGROUND

1 The Beginnings of the Indies

Columbus was at sea for exactly 32 days when land was sighted off San Salvador, early on 12 October 1492. Columbus' flagship, the *Santa Maria*, was a small carrack of about 150 tons burden. It was 75 feet long and had a 25-ft beam and a draught of six feet. It managed to survive the dangerous waters around the Bahamas islands, but ran aground off Hispaniola on Christmas Day 1492 and was abandoned. Columbus had no high opinion of his flagship. He called it a 'dull sailor and unfit for discovery'.

When Columbus arrived at San Salvador he believed that he had reached one of many islands off the coast of Japan. Later he believed that Cuba was Japan, the Cipango of Marco Polo, when he discovered it 15 days after his disembarkation at San Salvador. For Columbus the Bahamas were never more than gateways to the mainlands of the Indies and he never saw them twice. Like the other islands of the Indies which he was to discover on his next three voyages they were merely 'halting-places' on the way to Cathay, the terrestrial Paradise. The exciting project which the Spanish monarchs and bishops had entertained of converting all the men and women of the newly discovered lands to Christianity was prevented in the Bahamas by the failure of the early colonizers to settle upon any of them. For this reason probably King Ferdinand writing to Diego Columbus in 1509 called them the 'useless islands'. They were not to be useless for long!

After exhausting the supplies of labour from Hispaniola the Spaniards on Hispaniola obtained permission from the King to bring over 'idle people' from the Lucayan islands on the pretext that they 'would never become Christians there'. But, according to Las Casas, the Lucayans who believed they would meet the souls of their dead relatives in Hispaniola were quickly killed off by overwork or through drinking the sap of the bitter cassava soon after transportation. Others, according to a Spaniard who had travelled with Lucayans to Cuba, were crowded up to 500 deep below deck, and died of lack of food, unbearable thirst, heat, grief and overcrowding. According to this Spaniard there was not a single ship which went to attack the Indians of the Lucayan islands and of the mainland *which did not throw overboard one third or one quarter of those embarked*!

It may be stated without fear of contradiction that whoever eventually benefited from the discovery by Europeans of the Bahamas islands it was not the resident Lucayans. It is possible however that the days of the Lucayans in the islands might not have survived for long the attacks from hostile Indians who were coming from larger islands in the west or from the North American mainland. Las Casas writing in 1559 makes the wholesale depopulation of the islands seem worse by describing the Lucayans as surpassing all in the Indies and in the whole world 'in gentleness, simplicity, humility, peaceful disposition, tranquillity and in other virtues'. Perhaps they were all these things and more. We shall never know for certain. Oviedo noted another quality about them. Like the Indians of Terra Firma, the Lucayans were, he said, 'the largest people discovered up to now.' Oviedo spent more than ten years living amongst the Indians on the mainland and from his descriptions we get a fairly comprehensive picture of the kind of people they were and the sort of life they led. In many respects beside their stature the Lucayans must have been like them. First of all, Oviedo tells us, 'Indians built their villages near the sea and fished with very good nets made of cotton'. They used *barbacoas* or sticks placed over a pit to roast fish on the day of catching for 'fish and meat soon spoil if they are not roasted on the same day. . . .' He continues, 'The caciques and lords among the Indians take as many wives as they desire. The eldest son succeeds the father, or, if there is no son, the eldest daughter. Sons of second daughters take priority over daughters of first born sons as heirs. . . . The ordinary Indian men take only one wife and only divorce them sometimes if they are barren. For the most part women are virtuous, but there are some, especially high born women, who give themselves to any man who wants them. Only low born women refuse. . . .' Native women, says Oviedo 'are very fond

1 (*opposite*) *The beach at Governor's Harbour, Eleuthera*

The Life of Capt. AVERY.

HE was the fon of John Avery, a victualler, near Plymouth, who, in a few years, was grown as opulent in his purfe, as in his body, by fcoring 2 for 1; and when he had fo done, drink-

A 5
ing

2 'The Successful Pirate', Captain Avery

of the Spaniards and consider themselves highly honoured when they are loved by them. . . . When they become pregnant many of the Indian women eat of an herb that moves and expels the pregnancy . . . the young women do not want to give up their pleasures, or to become pregnant, because childbearing causes their breasts to become flabby. They have beautiful breasts and are quite proud of them. . . . In some places they wear a cloth wrap that reaches from the waist to the knees, covering their sexual members. The rest of the body is entirely naked. . . . The chiefs wear a tube of gold, and the other men large snail's shells, in which they place the male organ. The rest of the body is naked. . . .'

If Oviedo's testimony is to be believed, Indians behaved as badly on occasions as their European overlords. The differences over which the Indians quarrel and go to battle, he says, 'are concerning who shall have the most land and power. They kill those they can and sometimes they take captives whom they brand and keep as slaves. Each master has his own brand and some masters pull out one front tooth of their slaves as a mark of ownership. The bow-using Caribs, as the people of Cartagena, and most of those who live along the coast, eat human flesh. They do not take slaves, nor are they friendly to their enemies or foreigners. They eat all the men that they kill and use the women they capture, and the children that they bear—if any Carib should couple with them – are also eaten. The boys they take from foreigners are castrated, fattened and eaten. The Indians have special men whom they respect and call *tequina*. They call any man who excels in any art a tequina, whether he is the best hunter or fisherman or the best maker of nets, bows, or other things. . . . They also call tequina the one who is master of communications and intelligence with the devil. This tequina speaks with the devil and receives replies from him. He then tells the Indians what they must do and he predicts the future. Since the devil is an old astrologer, he knows what the weather will be . . . he informs them of the future and gives them to understand that through his deity, or as lord of all and mover of everything that is and will be, he can foresee things of the future . . . and that he causes the thunder, and makes the sun and rain, that he rules the weather, and that he gives and deprives them of food. The

B

Indians . . . believe everything he says and fear and respect him, and in certain places make sacrifices of blood and human lives. . . .

The natives say that the Tuyra really speaks to them. That is their name for the devil. In some places also they call Christians Tuyra, believing that by that name they honour and praise them.' In reality, notes Oviedo at this point, it is a proper name for some who have gone to the New World, who 'having cast aside their consciences and fear of either divine or human law, have done things characteristic not of Christians but of dragons and infidels. *Maliciously they have caused the death of many Indians who could have been converted and saved*. Even if those who died could not have been converted, they could have been useful to your Majesty (Charles v) and helpful to the Christians. And no part of the island would have been completely depopulated, for from the above cause it is almost uninhabited. Those who have perpetrated these crimes call the uninhabited places "peaceful". *I feel they are more than peaceful; they are destroyed*'.

It should be noted that the Bahamas islands were not the only ones to be depopulated by the Spaniards, who had exceeded the instructions and good intentions of the Catholic monarchs.

Oviedo describes several types of Indian dwellings. The walls of most were made of canes tied together with lianas and plastered over with earth four or five fingers thick. The roofs were of straw or long grass which were rainproof. Hammocks were used as beds, either outdoors tied to trees or indoors fastened between two posts. Hammocks were well woven cotton cloth of good and pretty tapestry and two or three yards long. They hung 'four or five palms from the ground like a sling or a swing.' Among Indians the principal men have designs on their arms and chests. Only slaves have them on their faces. Women wear bracelets with beads of shell and gold alternating above the ankles and below the knees. The principal women also wear strings of beads and other trinkets around their necks. They also wear gold rings in their ears and noses, with a hole made from one nostril to the other and the ring hanging down over their lips. Some Indians crop their hair although most wear it long. They are able to cut it very easily and evenly with floats. 'Women with sagging breasts support them with a rod of elaborately wrought gold about a palm and a half long . . . a small hole is drilled through each end, through which are fastened cotton cords. One end of the cord goes over the shoulder and the other under the arm pit where the two ends are tied'.

Beside fish and fruit Indians ate bread made from Indian corn or cassava, rat-like animals (hutias) and rabbits (conies) and iguanas. They made a wine or chicka drink from corn grains soaked for four days only.

'To build fires', says Oviedo, 'Indians select two of the lightest and driest sticks they can find and place them like two fingers held tight together. Between them they then place the point of a slick smooth hardwood stick which they twist rapidly between their palms by rubbing them back and forth. As the point of the "fire" stick wears into the other sticks on the ground they catch fire in a very short time. Indians are very expert in extracting salt from sea water. More than any people in the world they are inclined to barter, sell and trade. Their dugouts go from one place to another, and they carry salt where it is needed, and in exchange they receive gold or cloth or cotton thread, slaves, fish or other things'.

The Spaniards used Indians to dig and clear the earth from gold mines. The method of 'mining' was to fill trays with earth dug from the soil and to carry them alongside streams of water for 'panning'. Indians had become expert at gilding copper and base gold to look like 22 carat gold. They were also superb pearl fishers. Oviedo says that some could remain underwater an hour or more, which suggests that they had perfected some simple form of apparatus for breathing undersea!

The New World, which had scourges of its own before the arrival of European men and women, soon became a place of European conflict by land and sea. Distance from the centres of human society did not encourage European men and women to behave any better than they did at home.

While new human dramas were being enacted by conquistadores and settlers who continued to pierce deeper and deeper into the new continent and while sea-rovers, adventurers, explorers, privateers and corsairs ploughed distant oceans in their relentless search of 'short' routes to Asia or searched for treasures in the shape of gold and trade, the low sea-islands of the Bahamas if not entirely 'useless' were mostly neglected. Sailors avoided them as 'wrecking places' even though from earliest times ships put into their small natural harbours in search of water, salt, game, fruit and fish. They were useful too as ports in a storm. Some islands were relatively rich in gum trees and sassafras, or in ambergris, which was vomited by passing whales and later washed ashore on Bahamian beaches. But most islands were not much more than tiny specks on an ocean when compared to the larger islands of the Western Caribbean sea, the mainlands of the centre and south, or the long eastern seaboard of North America.

Spain was too powerful in Europe and overseas during most of the century which followed upon Columbus' discovery to be challenged directly by the emerging nations of England and France, although French and English sea-adventurers conducted frequent acts of piracy against Spanish ships and lands with varying degrees of success. Neither France nor England had a navy to spare for regular warfare in the Caribbean. Europe was torn by wars of religion for a hundred years between 1559 and 1659. Spain's decline as the mighty European power was well advanced by 1659, but in 1580, when Portugal was annexed, the size of the Spanish Empire was much too vast to be toppled by adventurers from the emerging maritime nations. Yet Spain's Armada against England was crushingly repulsed in 1588 and Elizabethan seamen were able to multiply their assaults upon Spanish treasure ships and Spanish American cities. Englishmen also began to hatch schemes of settlement upon lands which God's Regent on Earth, the Bishop of Rome, had reserved for Spain and Portugal. The earliest of these colonies were financed by gentlemen who had failed to establish permanent settlements in Ireland. The death knell of Spanish overlordship began to sound when seven provinces of Flanders led by Holland broke away from Spain in 1579 and proclaimed a federal republic in 1581. So harassing were the activities of this breakaway dominion for Spain that by 1609 she had to sue for a truce because Dutch sailors were making too many inroads into her colonies and were destroying her communications by sea. In 1621 the Dutch had formed a West India company to engage in acts of piracy and contraband, and followed up this act of aggression by putting down roots in Brazil and on the Hudson river in North America. Later they made Curaçao the centre for slaves brought over from Guinea and the base for Dutch corsairs who harassed Spanish ships. The English who had been helped by the Dutch during their resistance to Spanish invasion were no less slow to develop an appetite for settling upon overseas lands, which were technically Spanish but which they considered should now belong to whoever could "effectively occupy" them. English settlements began to be increasingly made in South and North America and by the end of the first quarter of the seventeenth century colonisation of Spanish possessions had spread to the lower Antilles, St Christopher being the first choice. It is hardly surprising that the scattered islands of the Bahamas, positioned irregularly off two large islands, Cuba, and Hispaniola and the Spanish mainland of Florida were not selected before the more fertile lesser Antilles or mainlands. Only Sir Robert Heath had thought enough of their potential value to have them included in the grant of Carolina which Charles 1 made to him in the autumn of 1629. However, as it turned out British contacts with the Bahamas continued to be made in the early seventeenth century largely by Bermudian sailors who passed along the islands on their way to and from settlements on the Eastern seaboard of North America.

One of the original members of the company for Plantation of the Somers Islands, as Bermuda was long called by the English, was Robert Rich Earl of Warwick. In 1647 when a former Bermudan governor William Sayle had formed a company in London to colonise Eleuthera, the Earl of Warwick for whom he had worked in Bermuda was still Lord High Admiral and Governor in Chief of all the islands and other plantations subject to the English Crown. Warwick was no longer in office when Parliament on 31 August 1649 passed 'an act' for the Adventurers for the Eleutherian islands, but it is reasonable to suppose that without his assistance Sayle and his associates would not have easily obtained proprietorship of islands which had been earlier granted to Sir Robert Heath.

Bermuda, which had been settled in the years of peace which James 1 had established with Spain soon after he succeeded Elizabeth on the throne, early came into conflict with Spanish authorities because of the 'piratical tendencies' of its colonists. In view of later Bahamian history it is interesting to reflect that the Eleutheran adventure and the New Providence settlement which followed much later in the mid 1660s both relied principally on recruits from Bermuda. Without the enterprising and experienced Bermudan adventurers it is possible that the Bahamas would not have been colonised until the eighteenth century.

New Providence was settled in the year when most of the City of London was destroyed by fire, when it was still reeling from the effect of the Great Plague and in the middle of the second war with the Dutch. It was not easy to find English-born settlers in such times for distant islands!

The Bermudan settlers had learnt before going to the Bahamas how to raise vegetables on limited soil, how to act as carriers between the islands and North America, how to rake and carry salt to the fisheries of New England and Newfoundland, how to 'fish for wrecks' and how to go privateering or as pirates. These occupations were to become predominant in the Bahamas later in the seventeenth century and to endure until well into the second quarter of the eighteenth.

Although the Adventurers had drawn up a most elaborate and seemingly attractive set of rules for running a small oligarchic society on Eleuthera and although some settlers were able to put down roots, the years immediately preceding the first Dutch War (1652–4) and the Great Western Design of Cromwell (1655) were not propitious for settlement of islands which lay in seas regarded by sailors as 'very rough, heady and dangerous'. The first settlers on Eleuthera did in fact suffer shipwreck and were forced to appeal to New Englanders on the mainland for help. In return for corn and other supplies they made their much publicised indirect gifts to Harvard in 1650 of ten tons of braziletto wood. By 1656, however, the settlement on Eleuthera was in such straits that Cromwell's Council commanded the officer in charge of newly captured Jamaica to take 60 English survivors from there and settle them on Jamaica. Before action could be taken the English had departed for Bermuda. William Sayle was back in London in 1658 commissioning agents to organise trade between Bermuda, Eleuthera, London and other places. Very few of his original adventurers remained on Eleuthera and jurisdiction over them seems to have been carried on, if at all, by authorities in Bermuda. The Bermudans must have considered they had some real claim to be called colonisers in the Bahamas for their Grand Jury made a petition in 1688 to the Privy Council in Britain demanding the annexation of New Providence.

By that time there had been considerable changes in Europe and the Bahamas. The year after Cromwell's death (1658), England and France made peace with Spain by the Treaty of Pyrenees. This year of 1659 may be regarded as a watershed in the history of European rivals for it marked the decline of Spain as the major world power and the emergence of France as a rival to Holland and England. Charles II was restored to the English throne in 1660. Under Clarendon's administration, which lasted until 1667, there was a flowering of colonial expansion which was encouraged by Privy Councillors who consulted mercantile opinions but sought to keep executive control of overseas territories firmly within their grasp. Their method was to continue to grant exclusive charters or monopolies, as for example were extended to the Levant, East India or Royal Fishery Companies in 1661, the Royal Company of Adventurers Trading into Africa in 1663, and the Canary Islands Company in 1665. In 1663, too, eight of the most powerful men in the kingdom received a Royal charter making them proprietors of hundreds of miles of American coastal lands stretching between Virginia and Florida. Six of these men, the Duke of Albermarle, the Earl of Craven, Lord Berkley, Lord Ashley, Sir George Carteret and Sir Peter Colleton were to become Lords Proprietors of the Bahamas, seven years later. Lord Ashley has been described by one historian as a hard-headed business man with a particular interest in his 'darling Carolina'. As early as 1646 he had bought a share in a Barbados plantation of 105 acres. He sold this share in 1965 for £1020. Five years after the grant of Carolina, Ashley, who was created Earl of Shaftesbury in 1672, invested £200 as founder's shares in a voyage undertaken by the Hudson Bay Company. He later increased his stock in the company and was appointed deputy governor in 1673, the year in which he fell from Royal favour.

Ashley was deeply involved with colonies from July 1660 when he served on the Privy Council's Standing Committee on Trade and Plantations. Later that year he became a member of the Council of Trade and a member of the Council of Foreign Plantations He also served on different committees of Parliament concerned with trade and plantations. In 1672, when the Council of Trade and Foreign Plantations were merged, Ashley became President. If anyone could make the Bahamas prosperous Lord Ashley seemed to be the man. This at least was the opinion of two settlers on New Providence, John Darrell and Hugh Wentworth. They wrote Ashley as Palatine of the Carolina Company recommending the Lords Proprietors to obtain a charter for developing the Bahamas along the same lines as they were adopting for the mainland territory. They particularly stressed the benefits to be obtained from growing 'good cotton' and 'gallant tobacco', and also recommended growing sugar cane, cultivating braziletto, hunting turtles and collecting ambergris. At the same time they pointed to the urgent needs on New Providence of small arms and ammunition to defend settlers from attacks by sea, and asked for a 'godly minister and a good smith'.

Ashley acted quickly. By November 1670 six of the Lords Proprietors of the Carolinas were granted 'the islands of the Bahamas, which lay in the degrees of twenty two and tweny seven N. latitude'. In return Charles II asked for himself, his heirs and successors the 'fourth part of all gold and silver ore which . . . shall from time to time happen to be found'. People from England or liege people of the English King anywhere else were encouraged to settle on the islands in order to defend them strongly from incursions of 'savages, other enemies, pirates and robbers'. In return Charles II promised to make their children and 'such as shall descend from them there born or hereafter to be born denizens and lieges of his, his heirs and successors of the kingdom of England'.

Since all Parliamentary acts from 1642 onwards were abolished by the 'Cavalier Parliament' which first met after the Restoration in 1661 and lasted till 1679, the Rump Parliament's Act of 1649 which gave proprietorship to William Sayle had become invalid. Nearly 100 years later, however, in 1768 the Privy Council upheld a claim made by Daniel Coxe under the Heath patent of 1629 and awarded 100,000 acres in New York as recompense.

Ashley's interests lay more in trade than in searching for gold and silver. In 1672 he formed a company whose shareholders included John Darrell and John Locke, the liberal philosopher who had written the Fundamental Constitutions of Carolina in 1669. Despite the energetic efforts to promote trade between settlers in the Bahamas and Spaniards in Cuba and Florida the company was not very successful, although John Locke did obtain £127 10s for his £100 shares of stock, when he sold out in 1676. Spain had made a commercial treaty with England in 1667, the year in which peace was signed with the Dutch at Breda, so Ashley's business efforts were carried on in a changed atmosphere which was to alter even more favourably in 1670 when Spain made official recognition for the first time of British sovereignty over their effective settlements in the Spanish Indies. The Spaniards had acted out of weakness. They were unable to suppress the buccaneers whom the British had actively encouraged during their third war against the Dutch in the West Indies. After the Dutch surrender at Breda the English no longer feared them as rivals in the Caribbean and were ready to consider suppresion of the buccaneers in the interests of the concessions they hoped to gain from Spain as suppliers of slaves and of other requirements to the Spanish colonists in America. Suppression was not made effective until the year 1682 when buccaneers returning from an expedition beyond Cape Horn were arrested as pirates by British authorities. Some years later the French also took stern measures against the buccaneers whom Colbert had encouraged in the West Indies. Ashley had fallen from Royal favour in 1673 and he spent the remaining years of his active life in organising political 'whig' opposition to the Royalist supporters of the Stuarts in Parliament. If Ashley had not fallen out of favour with the King he might have been able to prevent the Bahamas from being overrun by the lawless men who saw in their numerous cays, creeks, harbours, shallows, reefs and headlands ideal conditions for surprise attacks and escapes at sea. While the freebooting fraternity who had compelled the Spaniards to recognise British sovereignty in their Indies were transferring their headquarters from Tortuga to the Bahamas,

Charles II, their former patron, was busy creating a powerful colonial administrative machine in England. In 1675 he appointed nine Privy Councillors to the Lords Committee on Trade with the express purpose of ensuring obedience to the authority of the Crown. Gradually the power of the Privy Council was extended until in 1688 a committee of the whole Council was made responsible for the business of Trade and Foreign Plantations.

During years of colonial activity in England, which were remarkable for the extension of territory in America (Pennsylvania 1681, New Hampshire 1682) the Bahamas slipped backwards into lawlessness. As early as 1671 the first governor appointed by Ashley and his fellow Lords Proprietors reported that the men on New Providence 'neglected their crops' and preferred to run a 'coasting in shallops which is a lazy course of life and leaveth none but old men, women and children to plant'. So-called 'planters' in the southern islands of the Bahamas provoked the Spaniards on Cuba enough for them to attack them and carry them off to Havana in 1682. The Spaniards of the time never admitted the legality of British presence in the Bahamas. Two years later in 1684, because he was convinced that the people of New Providence were 'pirates proven', Cuba's Governor launched an attack upon the island and forced many persons to flee to Jamaica. Some also escaped to Massachusetts. For some years development in the Bahamas came to a standstill and it was not until 1687 when the Duke of Albermarle's exploration in the waters between Tortuga and the Turks Islands (at the extreme southern part of the archipelago) brought to light 26 tons of lost Spanish treasure that the Bahamas were once again on everyone's lips. Men talked about them with an excitement unequalled since Raleigh's search for the Golden Man (El Dorado). The atmosphere created by treasure hunting further encouraged piracy rather than agriculture and fishing as a means of livelihood for the island dwellers. John Oldmixon, whose knowledge of the Bahamas was based on reports given to him at secondhand by a former governor, described Nassau in 1708 as 'little more than a pirate's republic'. The people of Providence, Harbour Island and Eleuthera then dealt with wrecks, he wrote in the *History of the British Empire in America*, 'as it is said the good men of Sussex do. All that came ashore was Prize, and if a sailor had by better luck than the rest got ashore, he was not sure of getting off again'. According to Oldmixon, the people who had gone from England and other places to settle in the Bahamas had become impatient with government and lived a 'lewd, licentious life'. It is not clear what proportion of these settlers were active pirates, but when in 1688 instructions were given to Thomas Bridges as Governor for the Lords Proprietors he was explicitly told: 'you are not to suffer any Pyrats or Privateers to come into or be received at Providence or at any other of the islands of your government'. Bridges was empowered to govern through a Council which was fully representative of the proprietors' deputies and an assembly of 20 freeholders elected by all other freeholders. All laws passed by his Parliament were, however, to be sent back to England for approval. Bridges had returned to the Bahamas from Jamaica, but he seems to have been better suited to his Jamaican occupation of 'preacher'. In any event the 'revolution' in England that year was hardly conducive to firm action by a newly appointed governor.

Oldmixon quotes Thomas Bulkley for an account of the Bahamas under Cadwallader Jones who succeeded Bridges as governor in 1690. 'The inhabitants', wrote Bulkley, 'lived in abominable slavery', while Jones attempted to maintain himself in absolute unlimited power. Among the things he did, according to Bulkley, were the use of the royal style, conferring of honours and investment of persons with the privileges of peers in England, pardoning of capital offenders, the seizure and conversion of public treasure to his own use, neglect of defence, embezzlement of stores of powder, inviting of pirates to come to the port (of Nassau), refusal to take the oath to William and Mary upon taking office. Just how much Cadwallader Jones was friendly to pirates because they preferred James II to the new Dutch King is impossible for us to know with certainty, but it is evident from Bulkley's charges that he was much more of an opportunist than an impartial administrator. Bulkley was no less guilty of taking sides. He accuses Jones of wilfully neglecting to call an assembly for six months and of governing by orders of a Juncto. When finally the Assembly met he 'directed his son who was a captain of a ship in the Port to lay her so as to bring all her guns to bear upon the house where the General Assembly was sitting'. Bulkley also accused Jones of abruptly dissolving the Assembly and conspiring to banish some of the most virtuous and useful inhabitants. He also reproved him for saying that 'it was high treason to sign a petition for the sitting of a General Assembly'. 'One may see', wrote Bulkley, 'how petty plebeian tyrants agree with the sovereign imperial ones in their dread of parliaments'.

Bulkley, who was 'deputy secretary' in Nassau, accused Jones of high treason and had him imprisoned. But Jones had friends. On 27 February, 1692, according to Council's accusation against the Governor, we are told that 'some desperate rogues, pirates and others gathered together an ignorant seditious rabble, who with force of arms, rescued the Governor, proclaimed him again, and restored him to the exercise of his despotic power'.

The tables having been turned, Jones tried to get a packed jury from Harbour Island and Eleuthera 'to do Bulkley's business'. He was unsuccessful and Bulkley was acquitted by the new governor Nicholas Trott when he arrived to take over from Jones. Before Trott arrived, says Oldmixon, the use of Nassau to describe the principal town of New Providence was common. The town had 160 houses and was as big 'as the centre of St James' and St Mary's in Maryland and Virginia'. In Trott's time, there was a church in the town of Nassau, he began a fort in the middle of it, which with his house made a square. He mounted the fort with 28 guns and some demiculvers. Trott told Oldmixon that there never was a man-of-war at Providence unless 'Avery the pirate's ship may be reckoned one, for it carried 46 guns'. Trott said that they were only '70 men at that time upon the island both able and disabled and Avery had 100 stout men!' A little before and a little after, Trott told Oldmixon, there were 200 men, 'which was the greatest number that could ever be numbered in the Bahama islands'. Besides the settlements on New Providence there were others on Harbour Island and Eleuthera. Harbour Island had about 20 houses and Eleuthera less. There were two or three families on some other islands. Everyone went to Nassau to 'give their votes'. The Assembly consisted of 20 members but the governor was 'hard put to it for want of men'. Half the people was 'always upon guard at all times and duty was so long and came about so fast, the inhabitants were terribly fatigued'.

England had been at war with France since 1689 and Louis xiv did not recognise William iii as King of England until the conclusion of hostilities when peace was made at Ryswick in 1697. Five years earlier, however, the French fleet had been humiliated by the English navy in the channel off La Hogue. In the Bahamas the unsettled conditions of the time would have been responsible for the continuous watches which the relatively small number of people had to keep against surprise attack. Trott seems to have kept his copybook fairly clean as governor until the arrival of the pirate Avery on All Fool's Day 1696 off Royal island, north of Eleuthera. Avery had on board enormous loot captured in the Indian Ocean. Trott for whatever reason gave permission for the pirates to enter the port of Nassau. Outnumbered as he was he could hardly have done anything else, without risking the loss of his headquarters. The romance associated with piracy looks less appealing at close quarters. In the case of Avery there was little glamour even though his piratical deeds were acclaimed on the English stage. Actually Avery found it very difficult to dispose profitably of the Great Mogul's jewels and died in debt in Bideford.

Modern piracy may be traced back to the persecution of the Moors by the Spaniards. The alliances with Algerine pirates during European conflicts set precedents for behaviour in the Caribbean sea by European interlopers who wanted to challenge Spanish supremacy there. The buccaneers of the Caribbean sea in many respects resembled the corsairs of the Barbary ports of Algiers, Tunis and Tripoli but had less justification for turning pirates. Their activities were sometimes encouraged and often overlooked by the authorities of their countries who gained by the lawless attacks of the international sea rovers at the expense of their hated enemy Spain. From 1625, when smuggling began on St Christopher till 1685, when for the last time buccaneers defied Spanish defences in the bay of Panama, French and English sea-rovers continued the private war against Spain which had been started by the Dutch West India Company. As France replaced Spain as the greatest power in Europe and the navies of the maritime nations grew in strength the semi-official need for buccaneers diminished and public opinion turned against them. In times of war, however, sea-rovers continued to be commissioned as 'privateers' and they were used extensively by the Americans during the nineteenth century.

The pirates' historian, Captain Charles Johnson, whose volume first appeared in 1724, describes how pirates hoped to accumulate sufficient fortunes from raids in West Indian and North American waters to enable them to make foreign expeditions. 'The first is usually to Guinea, taking the Azores and Cape Verd islands in their way, and then to Brazil and the East Indies, where, if they meet with prosperous voyages they settle down at Madagascar or the neighbouring islands and enjoy their ill-gotten wealth among their elder brethren with impunity.' In his *History*, Johnson says that 'the Bahama islands were possessed by the English till the year 1700 when the French and Spaniards from Petit Guavas (in Haiti) invaded them, took the fort and Governor in the island of Providence, plundered and destroyed the settlements, etc., and carried off half the blacks and the rest of the people, who fled to the woods, retired afterwards to Carolina'.

He quotes an address from the House of Lords in 1705 to Queen Anne, which set forth: 'that the French and Spaniards had twice overrun and plundered the Bahama islands: that there was no form of government there; that the harbour of the island of Providence might be easily put in a posture of defence, and that it would be of dangerous consequence should these islands fall into the hands of the enemy'. But 'it happened' says Johnson, 'no means were used in compliance to that address for securing the Bahama Islands, till the English Pirates had made Providence their retreat and general receptacle. Then it was found absolutely necessary.' Accordingly George 1 in September 1716 made an order for a combined operation to be undertaken to suppress the pirates. Ships carrying 140 guns were to operate from Jamaica while others would assist from Barbados, the Leeward islands, New England, Virginia and New York. Two men-of-war were sent to the Bahamas with Captain Woodes Rogers, the man who rescued Alexander Selkirk from Juan Fernandez (Robinson Crusoe's island in the Pacific) and made enough money from his armed voyage around the world in 1708–11 to obtain a 21-year lease of the Bahama islands from the proprietors. Before Governor Rogers went over a Royal Proclamation promising pardon for pirates surrendering before 5 September 1718 had been sent to New Providence. The pirates captured the ship bearing the proclamation, but 'Captain Jennings who was their commodore, and who always bore a great sway among them, being a man of good understanding and a good estate before this whim took him of going a-pirating resolved upon surrendering without more ado to the terms of the Proclamation. . . . And presently Jennings and by his example about 150 more, came in to the Governor of Bermuda and had their certificates, though the greatest part of them returned again, like the dog to the vomit.

The commanders who were then in the island, besides Captain Jennings. . . . I think were there: Benjamin Hornigold, Edward Teach, John Martel, James Fife, Christopher Winter, Nicholas Brown, Paul Williams, Charles Bellamy, Oliver La Bouche, Major Penner, Ed. England, T. Burgess, Tho. Cocklyn, R. Sample, Charles Vane and two of three others. Hornigold, William Burgess and La Bouche were afterwards cast away; Teach and Penner killed and their crews taken; James Fife killed by his own men, Martel's crew destroyed and he forced on an uninhabited island; Cocklyn, Sample and Vane hanged; Winter and Brown surrendered to the Spaniards at Cuba, and England lives now at Madagascar.' The rewards for buccaneering were not necessarily great. As Captain Johnson put it, 'the far greater part of these rovers are cut short in the pursuit by a sudden precipitation into the other world'.

Woodes Rogers, who arrived in June 1718, was responsible for seeing that ten of them were so precipitated while 'four hundred of their sworn friends and companions' quietly stood by to behold the spectacle.

The Treaty of Utrecht 1713 had ensured that there would be no Spanish-French axis to prevent British expansion overseas and had given Britain the monopoly of supplying black slaves and of sending a yearly trading ship to the Spanish colonies in America. The importance of the Bahamas for the security of trade with the West Indies is underlined by Oldmixon in a later edition of his *History*. He notes that the Parliament of England did not think it 'unworthy of their care, as to defend it against both Spaniards and French who find its situation very convenient to annoy or befriend their commerce'. Oldmixon records that Rogers brought with him above 100 soldiers, and formed three companies of militia who took turn in the fort while other soldiers looked after 8 guns mounted at the eastern entrance to the harbour. Negroes carried out repairs to Fort Nassau and erected another one at the harbour's mouth. They also cleared the surrounding grounds of bushwood and shrubs and palisaded the forts which were kept in 'good condition and very defensible'. Oldmixon considered that a force would always be necessary because the Spaniards and the French looked upon possession of the islands by the English with an envious eye, 'not for the beauty of the country nor the fertility of the soil but for the commodiousness of their situation to annoy and distress them in their navigation'.

Keeping a force happy was another matter. The independent company recruited for the defence of Nassau mutinied in 1736, not surprisingly in Oldmixon's judgement, 'their whole design being only to get from a place where the pay is scarce sufficient for them here (Nassau) as in Jamaica and other places'. Rogers' defences of Nassau proved adequate in 1720 when a Spanish force attacked in February, unaware of the peace which had been concluded at Aix the month before. By 1721 Rogers had worn himself out and decided to seek help first from Carolina where he ordered a supply of provisions before returning to England. Instead of the assistance he looked for he was imprisoned for debt.

While Rogers was languishing in an English prison or was recovering from his strenuous exertions in Nassau a certain George Phenney was holding the fort in the Bahamas. His wife, however, seems to have usurped his authority for she is accused of cornering the market in salt and other commodities and to have frequently 'brow beaten jurys and insulted even the justice on the Bench'. Woodes Rogers returned to the Bahamas on 25 August 1729. He came soon after a hurricane and found the Fort in bad condition. Furthermore he got little support from the Assembly which had finally been authorised in his commission after continuous petitions made during the régime of George Phenney. It had

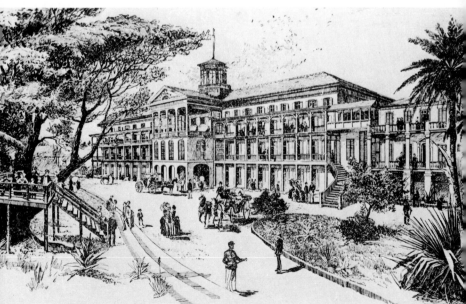

3 (top) *Nassau in the Age of Sail*
4 (above) *The Royal Victoria Hotel, 1891*

5 (left) First Earl of Shaftesbury

6 (right) Christopher Columbus

7 Woodes Rogers and his family by Hogarth

been urged in a petition of 10 April 1727 that a 'great reason' for there not being more inhabitants in the Bahamas was the 'want of an Assembly to compose a body of laws suitable to the circumstances of the colony'. Rogers was empowered to call an assembly consisting of 24 members to be chosen by a majority of the inhabitants on the basis of eight for Nassau, four for the Eastern district, four for the Western district (of New Providence) and four each for Eleuthera and Harbour Island. The experiment was a disappointment. Rogers dissolved the House on 8 December 1730 on the ground that it 'frequently met and made several resolves without doing anything to promote His Majesty's service or the welfare of the Colony'. This first new model assembly, and others which followed it, met in private houses. On occasions the Court House over the gaol was also used. It was not until 1815 that the House moved into its present chamber. Rogers received much opposition from the Speaker of the Assembly, John Colebrooke, who was prosecuted and fined but whose supporters continued to make life difficult for him until his death in 1732.

Richard Fitzwilliam, who bought the site of today's Government house from the Speaker of the House of Assembly, was less successful as governor than Rogers. Among his problems was an alleged Negro insurrection, an actual mutiny by troops, recalcitrant Assemblymen, shortage of provisions and his own conviction that the people on New Providence were 'beasts of burthen' fit only to be ruled with a 'rod and iron'. He lasted from mid-1734 till early 1738, when he was recalled to London. By 1738 warlike noises were once more being heard in England against Spanish insolence, as exemplified by guardacostas whom the English considered as no better than pirates. Between 1713 and 1731 no less than 180 English ships were said to have been molested by these Spanish watch-dogs against smugglers. In 1731 an Englishman, Captain Jenkins, had his ear torn off. The House of Commons expressed its anger forcibly when they heard of Jenkins' experience in 1738 and expressed a determination to protect their prized West Indian possessions more fully by offering to complete the purchase of the 'strategic Bahama islands' from the proprietors. The war which broke out with Spain in 1739 was from England's point of view to be fought in the West Indies. A new note of appreciation of colonists now begins to be heard in London. They are called very good men'. At least that is how Lord Cathcart, Commander Designate of the West Indies expedition, described them to the Duke of Newcastle in 1740. New attitudes to colonies resulted in the choice of new men to administer them. John Tinker, a son-in-law of Martin Bladen of the Board of Trade, seems to have been appointed Governor of the Bahamas more because of past experience than because of his special access to the corridors of power. He had worked for the South Sea Company in Portobello and Panama and was recommended by Bladen to Newcastle because he was a person of 'substance and experience in trade'.

Tinker reached the Bahamas on 21 April, 1741. It is indicative of the new firm policy in England that he should have travelled out with a military engineer sent out by the government to make Nassau 'the strongest possession in British America'. The engineer was Peter Henry Bruce, who had served in the Prussian and Russian armies before settling as a farmer in Scotland in 1724. Bruce, in his memoirs published in London in 1782, tells how he found the wooden Fort Nassau ready to tumble down. There was not a single mason on the island, but he collected 54 guns which he mounted on new carriages brought from England. New Providence's defences were not entirely hopeless. Because the island was 'so entirely surrounded by innumerable sunken rocks' it was impossible 'for any ship to land except in the harbour, and if an enemy were to land in boats it would be impossible for them to get through the underwoods, without cutting a road through them'. From Bruce we learn that many Palatines arrived in New Providence during the régimes of Rogers and Phenney, and by their 'industry and improvements upon their plantations, furnished the markets with all sorts of provisions'. Under the 'arbitrary and tyrannical' rule of Richard Fitzwilliam, says Bruce, the 'best of the inhabitants and all the Palatines withdrew from the island'. Bruce made building lime locally and by the end of July 1742 had completed Fort Montagu and Bladen's sea battery. In an effort to consolidate Bruce's work Tinker wrote to England asking for a supply of powder and small arms, a garrison of not less than 300 men, reinforcements for Fort Montagu where one officer and 50 men were required for ordinary guard duties, and £2,500 to complete renovations at Fort Nassau. He tried to strengthen his request by adding 'if the Spaniards succeed at Georgia, they will fall upon us next'. Bruce left New Providence for Charlestown, Carolina in 1745, after completing Fort Nassau and its sea battery. His military appreciation of the Bahamas generally was that they were more conveniently situated for 'annoying the Spaniards in time of war than any of our other settlements'. He considered that the Bimini islands, where the people of New Providence catch most of their tortoises and are frequently taken and carried prisoners to Havana, would be the 'most advantageous station in all British America' during a war, not least because 'Spanish homeward bound ships generally take in wood and water there'.

Bruce was not only interested in the arts of defence. He was unhappy that only New Providence, Harbour Island and Eleuthera were inhabited and that the total Bahamian population, white and black, men, women and children only totalled 2,300. It is very much to be làmented', he wrote, 'that these fertile and valuable islands should be uncultivated for want of people, which are capable of maintaining many thousands of families with ease: but it will ever be the case, while the governors are suffered to tyrannise over the inhabitants, as nobody that can do better will ever come to settle here, and of consequence, they must remain uninhabited'. As for the inhabitants already there, Bruce says 'it is their own fault' if they 'want any of the necessaries of life: they have horses, cows and sheep, goats, hogs and all sorts of poultry, but they neither sow nor plant more than is necessary for maintaining their own families; whereby one of the most fertile parts of our West Indies is neglected for want of cultivation. They depend on their cargoes of salt, mahogany, dyeing wood, tortoises, fruit, etc which they sell to great advantage; and likewise upon the shipwrecks which happen frequently upon these extensive banks'. On the other hand Bruce was careful to point out some of the inconveniences of life on the islands. The greatest 'they have here is from the plague of numerous vermin or insects, which torment them both night and day; as bugs, cockroaches, mosquitoes, flies, sandflies, ants and trigers (chigoes) . . . the mosquitoes and sandflies come in good swarms in the evening from the woods'. Even today's modern insecticides have not entirely banished unwanted vermin and insects, but the battle is being engaged and hopefully will be won.

During the years of the war of the Austrian succession crews of privateer ships who used Nassau's Vice Admiralty Court gave the town a taste of artificial prosperity by high spending on drinks, fees and other activities. After the treaty of peace was signed in 1748, however, there was a reversion to older methods of survival on the islands which Bruce had considered to be of such vital importance for British defence in America, and potentially valuable because of their natural resources. War with the French in 1756 was to release another outburst of privateering activity which, according to Governor Tinker, 'extinguished every other industrious or commercial application'. French involvement on the continent in support of Austria, and Prussia's alliances with England gave the English opportunities to hit hard at the French overseas empire. French possessions in the Caribbean, America and India fell to the superior forces organised by the vigorous William Pitt of England and Bahamian defences were not needed to protect the British fleet which captured Havana in 1762. This victory had followed upon continuous victories over French West Indian islands beginning with the fall of Guadeloupe in 1659, the *annus mirabilis* which witnessed the destruction of the French navy in Quiberon Bay and the expulsion of the French from Canada.

One English visitor to the Bahamas early in the eighteenth century would have rejoiced greatly at the fall of Havana and the destruction of one third of the Spanish navy there. After a visit to Carolina, Florida, Georgia and New Providence which lasted between 1722 and 1726 Mark Catesby wrote a *Natural History* in which he praised the refreshing winds of the north side of Cuba, particularly around Havana. To these winds, no doubt, wrote Catesby, 'is owing the healthiness of the air and good character of that proud emporium, the conquest of which by British arms would put us in possession of a country much more agreeable to British constitutions than any of the islands between the tropics, and under God enable them to multiply and stand their ground without the necessity of such numerous recruits from their mother country'.

From Catesby, whose illustrations of Bahamian and Carolinian flora, fauna and marine animals are priceless records for the student of natural history, we learn that the 'sickly inhabitants of the Carolina' early retired to the Bahama islands which are 'blest with a most serene air and are more healthy than most other countries in the same latitude'. Catesby also records that sugar cane was formerly planted, of which rum and molasses were made but was given up as soil fertility declined. In 1725 he found only a few houses in Nassau of stone, most of them being 'built with palmetto leaves'. He describes the occupations of the people as those of building ships, carrying salt to Jamaica and Hispaniola and of supplying Carolina with salt, turtle, oranges and lemons. A great number of the inhabitants of the Bahama islands in these years lived by hunting iguanas which Catesby called 'guanas'. They visited many of the 'remote cays and islands in their sloops to collect them, which they do by dogs trained up for that purpose, which are so dextrous as often not to kill them'. Any killed were put aside for immediate consumption, the others had their mouths sewn up to prevent them biting and were collected in the hold of the sloop, for carrying alive for sale to Carolina. Others were salted and barrelled up for the use of their families at home.

Before Havana fell George III had ascended the English throne. Pitt resigned a year later in 1761 and the young king tried to govern through a party of friends led by the Eard of Bute. In a mood of conciliation and hope that France and Spain would be appeased the British plenipotentiaries arranged in the Treaty of Paris for Havana to be restored to the Spanish in exchange for Florida and for the return of all the valuable West Indian islands to France. During the negotiations in Paris a French diplomat noted that if any possession could enable the British to intercept the Flota,* it was the Bahama islands, but that they had never been used for this purpose. The great imperial destiny which Bruce had claimed for the islands was doomed to failure, al-

---

* The Flota or Spanish Convoy made two trips annually between Spain and its American possessions. One of these convoys passed between Florida and the islands of Bimini on the homeward journey.

though on several future occasions the Bahamas were to be utilised for the benefit of wars in which the British were to be involved.

2 Growth and Development

It was less than a year after the Treaty of Paris that the French, under Comte d'Estaing, felt strong enough to challenge British sea power in the Caribbean by occupying Grand Turk. D'Estaing's departure from the island in November 1764 was due to diplomatic exchanges conducted through the Privy Council in England and not to British naval action. A consequence of the French intrusion was a British directive to Governor William Shirley of the Bahamas to take the Turks islands more firmly under the government of the Bahamas. This William Shirley was the man who had planned the capture of Louisburg in 1745 when he was Governor of Massachusetts. Shirley's name is fittingly perpetuated in a main street of Nassau because of the initiatives he took in reclaiming swamp lands preparatory to the extension of the town eastwards.

On Shirley's younger brother Thomas fell the burden of dealing with the troublesome Turks Islanders, who were only partially satisfied with Bahamian overlordship even when, with the Caicos islands, they were granted representation in the House of Assembly at Nassau in 1799. So neglected were the Bahamas on the eve of the great American rebellion that Shirley reported in 1773 that revenues were 'almost annihilated, the Treasury exhausted and the Courts of Justice have long been shut up'.

Under such conditions and led by a colourless governor Montfort Browne, the residents of New Providence showed no anxiety to resist the capture of Nassau by the American commodore, Ezekiel Hopkins, who appeared at daybreak off the bar on 3 March, 1776. During the two weeks in which the Grand Union flag flew over Bahamian forts and Government House in Nassau, Hopkins and his officers were 'elegantly entertained at the houses of some of the officers of the Government'. When Hopkins sailed on March 17 he took in his ships 88 cannon, more than 11,000 cannon balls and over 5,000 shells. When Governor Browne was able to return to Nassau in 1778 he found that many of the residents had left to join the rebel army in North America and that Nassau had experienced a second invasion of American marines in January of that year.

The 'acting Governor' of the Bahamas, John Gambier, requested permission from Browne to continue a license he had issued to the local merchants 'to carry on an open and free intercourse with the rebels under the pretext of procuring provisions'. Browne's attempt to restore British authority over New Providence was described in the following year by the Council of the Bahamas in a letter of protest to the Board of Trade as 'a state of absolute anarchy'. Browne was replaced in 1780 by John Maxwell.

For a period Nassau was used as a base by privateers who brought in no less than 127 rebel ships and more American prisoners than the authorities could accommodate or feed. Eventually a combined force of American and Spanish ships led by Cuba's Governor Don Juan de Cargigal invaded Nassau and persuaded Governor Maxwell to sign articles of surrender on 7 May 1782. A Spanish Governor, Don Antonio Claraco, then took over the administration of the Bahamas. Spain had been persuaded by France to join the war which had long ceased to be one exclusively concerned with independence for colonists in America and had become merged in a European effort to overthrow the British Empire. In 1780 the Dutch had joined Britain's enemies and the same year saw Russia, Prussia and the Scandinavian countries adopt a state of armed neutrality. The British Empire hovered critically on the brink of destruction. The British Commander in the English Channel, Sir Charles Hardy, had only 37 ships of the line to put against the combined French and Spanish fleet of 64. In the following year, 1781, the superior French fleet commanded by the Comte de Grasse cut British communications and compelled Lord Cornwallis to surrender at Yorktown. British command of the American seas was temporarily lost and the victory of the American rebels over Britain assured by this action. It was not until the spring of 1782, when on April 12 Admiral Rodney triumphantly prevented De

Grasse's fleet from reaching Jamaica by his victory near the Isles des Saintes in the Guadeloupe channel, that a new lease of life was gained by the British Empire elsewhere than in rebel America. Later in the year (September-October) General Elliott successfully resisted a combined Franco-Spanish invasion of Gibraltar. The recrudescence of British naval power was interestingly foreshadowed by the attack, though unsuccessful, of Horatio Nelson against the French force which had again seized the Turks islands in 1783.

When the preliminaries of peace were signed at Versailles between England and France on 20 January 1783 it was agreed in Article v that the King of Spain would 'restore to Great Britain the islands of Providence and the Bahamas without exception in the same condition in which they were conquered by the arms of the King of Spain'. Learning that East and West Florida were to be returned to Spain, Andrew Deveaux, an officer of the Royal Foresters of South Carolina then living in exile at St Augustine, did not wait for the formal signing of the Peace Treaty on 3 September 1783, but set out earlier for the Bahamas with a 'handful of ragged militia' in two brigantines. At Harbour Island he was joined by some settlers and Negro slaves before sailing for Nassau. Under cover of darkness Deveaux and his men overpowered the sentry on duty at Fort Montagu and got control of the soldiers who were asleep inside. Although Deveaux's force probably did not exceed 225 men he was able to give an impression of a much larger body by continuous rowing of the same men ashore and by returning them in a supine condition to their vessels. Some of the men were also painted to resemble Indians. As Deveaux had captured the ridge overlooking the fort and had given samples of his fire power the Spanish governor needed little persuasion to anticipate a withdrawal from the Bahamas which would in any event have taken place in accordance with the terms of the Treaty.

By his initiative and enterprise in being the first Loyalist to seek profits in the Bahamas, Deveaux obtained 250 acres of land on New Providence and 1,000 on Cat Island. The Harbour islanders also gained from their support of Deveaux because he took early opportunity to persuade the new Bahamian legislature that special rights of farming on Eleuthera should be granted to them. These rights have been maintained to this day. The Loyalist invasion of the Bahamas did not reach full flood immediately after the signing of the Peace Treaty. The British government continued for some time to retain armed posts in the American West, British merchants sought to collect pre-Revolutionary debts and Loyalists did all they could to recover pre-Revolutionary property. Congress had encouraged this persistence in fact agreeing in the peace treaty to make 'earnest recommendation' to the states to recover confiscated Loyalist property to its former owners. Once it was clear to the Loyalists that most states intended to ignore this recommendation there was nothing to keep them in America. The majority therefore took refuge in Canada, but some cotton planters of the South preferred the prospects of transferring their easy way of life and their slaves to the underdeveloped islands of the Bahamas.

Within five years the population of the Bahamas nearly trebled and the number of slaves rose from 50 to 75 per cent of the people resident on the islands. The decision of Loyalists to go to the Bahamas was encouraged by the authorities in England. A survey conducted by John Wilson in 1783 urged the need of people to develop the Bahamas and a royal proclamation of 1783 proclaimed the intention of the Crown to buy the islands from the Proprietors. Special incentives were also offered to Loyalists. They were to get lands 'free of charges' and were to be exempted 'from the burdens of the quit rents for ten years from the making of the grant'. Loyalist settlers were also to be taken to the Bahamas in ships provided at British expense. Most of the Loyalists went to the Bahamas in the years 1784–5. In the latter year all persons of English blood were advised to leave Florida for the Bahamas before the Spanish governor took formal possession of that country. Some of these Loyalists left Florida with regret.

Tensions between the Loyalist newcomers and the older inhabitants on New Providence were not slow to develop. The Loyalists who went to the 'Out islands' and took to farming were desirable immigrants, but the displaced persons who stayed in Nassau increased the problems of the administration. Governor Maxwell, in a report sent to London in 1784, spoke of 'officers, merchants and people who hope to return to the continent after peace there . . . they demanded everything immediately . . . in fact they almost wish to take over the government'.

After the Home government had refused his request for a regiment and ships to assist him in keeping Loyalists under control, Governor Maxwell embarked for England early in 1785. Over 100 Loyalists then signed a message in the *Bahamas Gazette* (first published in 1784) referring to 'Mr Maxwell's return to this Country as the greatest evil that can possible befall these Islands'.

The House of Assembly which had been convened by Governor Maxwell shortly before he left for England contained for the first time members for Exuma, Abaco, Long Island, Andros and Cat Island. Dissatisfied with their failure to obtain a majority the Loyalist members of the House withdrew from the Assembly. When later they circulated a protest against the election results the Speaker ordered a copy of it to be burnt by the hangman outside the Courthouse door. The passage of time and the expulsion of the Loyalist members for contempt and non-attendance in the House was the answer of the old Assembly members to the Loyalist bid for power. They were supported by the acting Governor James Powell. Neither Powell nor his successor in office favoured new elections. The antagonism between old settler and new Loyalist was accordingly allowed to work itself out without the aid of publicised party dissensions in the Assembly, which met only infrequently during a life which lasted until 1794.

Cotton exports rose from 124 tons in 1785 to 219 in 1787, but the most spectacular change in the Bahamian economy was to derive from the granting of Free Port status to Nassau in 1787. Under the British Act of that year seven free ports were designated in the Caribbean (one in the Bahamas, four in Jamaica, one in Grenada and one in Dominica). The aim of the new British legislation was to achieve an extension of British trade overseas, to acquire raw materials needed for Britain's expanding industries and to obtain maximum cargoes for Britain's merchant ships. The Anglo-French commercial treaty of 1786 had been the first step taken by Britain towards freedom of trade and was immediately beneficial to British cotton, hardware and pottery exports. The abandonment of mercantilism and protectionism was a natural consequence of the new thinking which since 1763 tended to regard British colonies more as markets for British produce than as sources of supply. The trend towards liberalisation of trade clearly benefited the Bahamas, for exports in the financial year 1786-87 rose to a record of £58,707 while imports increased to £136,359. A new era of prosperity seemed to be dawning for the Bahamas when in 1787 the Crown at last bought out the Proprietors by giving £2,000 each to the heirs of the six original Proprietors. Unfortunately, while British trade benefited from the use of Nassau's free port an insect, the Chenille bug, had started to play havoc with the cotton crop on the islands where production fell dramatically in 1788. The brief era of cotton plantation on the Out islands did not end until the abolition of slavery, but as early as 1805 several planters gave up the struggle against soil exhaustion and insect pests.

In October 1787 John Murray, Earl of Dunmore arrived to take up his appointment as Governor. The 4th Earl of Dunmore had succeeded to the title in 1756. In 1770 he had been appointed Governor of New York and later became governor of Virginia. During the American rebellion the Earl had transferred his seat of government to the *Fowey* man-of-war lying off Yorktown and collected a small fleet of ships around it for his protection. Later he took refuge on Gwynn's island on the Chesapeake river. He returned to England after he was dislodged from the island on 8 July, 1776. From then until his arrival in the Bahamas he attended meetings of the House of Lords, but did not hold any official position in the United Kingdom. The Earl had proclaimed freedom to all negroes who rallied to his standard during the American rebellion and may possibly have been selected by the Home authorities as a person of forward-looking views, at a time when there was agitation against the slave trade. Dunmore, however, had learnt little from his experiences as Governor of New York and Virginia and quickly fell out with the local power élites in the Bahamas.

William Wyly, his solicitor general, described him as 'obstinate and violent by nature . . . little cultivated by education, ignorant of the constitution of England'. He was also reprimanded for appointing to offices 'bankrupts, beggars, blackguards and the husbands of his whores'. Whatever the truth about these accusations, there is no doubt that Dunmore practised nepotism and exceeded his authority by appointing one of his sons to be lieutenant-governor. He also acquired a great deal of Bahamian land for himself. Through his failure to get on with the House of Assembly, Dunmore found it impossible to obtain adequate sums for administering the government. In 1793 the House refused to permit either the Governor or Council to see the vouchers or accounts upon which the Appropriation Bill had been passed. Earlier, in 1768, the House had shown awareness of its growing power by bringing the Reverend George Tizzard to its bar 'for reflecting on the Legislative bodies in a sermon preached by him', but their action against Governor Dunmore in 1793 effectively meant that they intended to be responsible for spending the taxpayers' money. Dunmore was forced to accede to their request on 10 September 1793 when he signed their Bill, but the House's right to control the budget was not formally admitted until 1828.

Dunmore, who had been actively engaged as a soldier in the American rebellion seems to have anticipated the violence which the French revolution was to unleash in the West Indies. Nothing else seems to justify his expenditure on forts and barracks. Fort Charlotte was actually begun two years before the Fall of the Bastille, but the barracks around it were not completed until a year after Britain was involved in the French Revolutionary war. When war broke out in 1793 Dunmore built batteries at Winton, on Hog Island and Potter's Cay and began construction of Fort Fincastle. On Harbour Island, where his name is commemorated still in Dunmore Town, and where the Earl had a summer house, Barracks Hill was provided with a fortification. There was real danger of enemy action against the Bahamas for the French Girondists had sent Edmond Genet to America as their envoy in 1792 with instructions to organise expeditions to detach Louisiana and Florida from Spain and to fit out American privateers to prey on British shipping. But for the Neutrality Proclamation by President George Washington the Bahamas might have needed Dunmore's forts.

When the Earl was ordered to return to England by the Duke of Portland in 1796, he was succeeded as acting governor by the Loyalist landowner from Exuma, John Forbes. This gentleman, who had accused Dunmore of favouring the lower order of whites, 'the descendants of pirates' died in the same fateful year which is still remembered in Bahamian annals for its terrible hurricane and outbreak of yellow fever.

Despite the decline of cotton growing the years of the war with revolutionary France and Napoleon seem to have been advantageous to the Bahamian economy. A census return in 1810 shows that the population had then reached 16,171 of whom nearly one fourth were white and the rest free people of colour and slaves. Imports for the year were £108,000 and exports were little short of half a million. According to a description published in 1819 in London cotton, salt, mahogany, dyeing woods, turtle and various sorts of fruit were then the chief exports of the islands. Most of the salt was obtained from the Turks Islands which were visited annually by between 1,000 and 2,000 salt rakers. The maritime people of the Bahamas were also said to 'derive considerable profit from following the business of wreckers, which consists in giving assistance to those who are wrecked, or in danger of being so, upon the almost endless rocks and shoals by which these islands are surrounded. This occupation employs an amazing number of vessels, no less than forty sails having been watching at one time off the Florida shore'. This account of wrecking published in the 1819 edition of the reprinted history, civil and commercial of the British West Indies by Bryan Edwards is sharply at variance with the account given by a visitor in 1803. In a conversation with a Bahamian 'conch' he was told that the forty sails off the 'Florida shore' were not there for 'humanity', but for 'racking'.

The author of the report which was published in Edward's *History* in 1819 also observed that the inhabitants of the Bahamas then had 'none of that attachment to the natal soil which is so strong in the people of most other countries' and quoted a report of 1815 drawn up by the House of Assembly which reported that the colonial attachments of the Bahamas were almost purely political, 'having little or no connection with any partial prejudices in favour of the soil, or any solid or immovable interest. The inhabitants for instance possess no extensive sugar works, or other manufactories. In the town of Nassau alone are to be found buildings of any value. From the necessity which the planters are under frequently shifting their residence from one tract to another, even their dwelling houses are but negro-huts upon a larger scale, composed of the same materials, and built and finished, and sometimes even furnished by the hands of the same rude artists. Should, therefore, his political attachments ever become shaken, the planter might remove, with as light a heart, and as little personal inconvenience, to a foreign island, as to one within the limits of the same government. Nor from the singular intricacy of the navigation of these numerous islands and circumjacent banks and keys, would it be an easy task to intercept him on his return'.

Conditions in England and in North America during the first decades of the nineteenth century were not favourable for inducing high motives in the people of the Bahamas. Britain was locked until 1815 in a grim struggle with the Napoleonic Empire and did not hesitate to stop and search American ships at sea, to impress seamen who were technically British subjects and to provoke the Americans to a Non-Intercourse Act in 1809 which closed American ports to British ships. This American defiance of Britain was particularly embarrassing at a time when Napoleon's continental system had left the United States as England's only large customer for manufactures. Impressment of men from American ships, hovering of British men of war around American ports, 'blockades' and orders-in-council finally persuaded Madison to declare war against Britain in 1812. The American navy was no match, however, for the British at this time. Whereas the British had 11 large warships, 34 frigates and 52 smaller warships in American waters the United States had only 16 ocean-going warships altogether including only three frigates. Under such circumstances the British could keep the American navy bottled up, but could not restrain the 500 American privateers then roaming the seas. Before hostilities ended in 1814 these privateers had captured more than 1,300 British merchantmen with cargoes valued at about $40 million. By comparison the 246 vessels condemned in the Vice Admiralty Court in Nassau between 1812–14 must appear trifling, although the profits deriving to some of the residents were not inconsiderable. The major significance of the struggle between Britain and France for the Bahamas and indeed for the world was to be the reality of British sea power. Never again would there be danger of invasion from any foreign power, and whatever decisions were later made about the future of the Bahamas at the centre of Empire could be upheld by force of arms if necessary. The first major decision of the United Kingdom was the abolition of the slave trade which hindsight now shows to have been inevitable ever since the judgement of the Earl of Mansfield in 1772 that slaves enjoyed the benefits of freedom while they stood on English soil. There could no more be pockets of slavery within an Empire than there could be first or second class citizens, as the spirit of Reform spread among the enlightened rulers of the British establishment in the nineteenth century. No longer were governors to be recalled from the Bahamas for daring to stand up to selfish local politicians who had learnt from eighteenth-century parliaments in Britain how to manipulate legislatures and courts of 'justice' to approve their particular programmes of profit making. The Emancipation Act, which was passed into law on 1 August 1833 in the Bahamas, was introduced by the Governor-in-Council at a time when the disapproving House of Assembly had been dissolved. When the Assembly was again reconvened the acting governor merely explained to it that public opinion in England had been responsible for the new measure. The real ending of slave conditions did not take effect until July 1838 when apprenticeship was terminated in the Bahamas and elsewhere in the British Indies. Thereafter only persons in a state of 'freedom' were to be residents of the Bahamas. Not all the freed slaves had originated within the boundaries of the islands. As late as the spring of 1838 over a thousand negroes were freed from a slave ship and brought ashore by seamen of the British Navy which had maintained a special squadron to suppress the traffic ever since the effective abolition of the trade by Britain in 1807. Some freed Africans arrived in the Bahamas as late as 1840 after being saved from slavery in the southern states of America by British sailors. Among settlements especially laid out for freed slaves were Grant's Town, Carmichael and Adelaide on New Providence, Williamstown and Victoria in the Berry Islands, Bennett's Harbour on Cat Island, the Bight and Great Harbour on Long Island and the harbours of Rum Cay and the Ragged Islands.

Slavery, if Daniel McKinnen who wrote in 1803 is to be believed, did not weigh as heavily upon its victims in the Bahamas as it did in other parts of America. 'The negroes of the Bahama islands', he wrote, 'discover, in general, more spirit and exertion

8 *On the road to Fort Montagu, 1891*

9 *Bay Street, Nassau, at the time of the American Civil War*

than in the southern parts of the West Indies. Something perhaps may be attributed to a more invigorating climate as a physical cause: but I believe more is due to the circumstances in which they are placed. Their labour is allotted to them daily and individually, according to their strength; and if they are so diligent as to have finished it at an early hour, the rest of the day is allowed to them for amusement of their private concerns. The master also frequently superintends them himself and therefore it rarely happens that they are so much subject to the discipline of the whip as where gangs are large, and directed by agents or overseers'.

Slaves had of course been set free by their masters as early as 1784 and between 1819–34 no less than 500 such freedoms are said to have been recorded. When a roll call of 10,110 slaves was made for the purposes of compensation in 1834 there were less than 1,000 slave owners in the islands. Of these only 11 were in possession of over 100. The owner of the largest number was the first Baron Rolle of Steventon, who seems never to have visited the Bahamas but who was active in British politics and civic affairs and was a liberal benefactor to the church. Rolle's name is the best known in Great Exuma today because he bequeathed his extensive lands on that island to be held in common for ever by all his slaves and their descendants.

The mould of post-slavery Bahamas was fashioned by Colonel William Colebrooke, who administered the government between 1835 and 1837. He reformed the magistracy, appointed constables in every district to act as advisers to apprentices, arranged for sketches and surveys of lands in the Out-islands, compiled analyses of soil fertility and made a start with school buildings and appointments of persons to promote education. Under Colebrooke's régime general court circuits were introduced to meet twice yearly in the Western Districts of the Berries, Biminis, Andros, Abaco, Grand Bahama and Harbour Island, the middle districts of Eleuthera, Long Island, Rum Cay, Exuma, Cat Island (then called San Salvador), Watling's island (the real San Salvador) and Ragged Island and the Eastern districts of Turks and Caicos and Inagua. Colebrooke was opposed in his reform of Bahamian society by the traditional old-style House of Assembly members whose views were championed in a newspaper published by a young American. Colebrooke regarded them as a faction, filled

D

with the spirit of 'Americanism', and lacking in reverence for royalty and of attachment to the mother country. The House of Assembly, it should be noted, had four coloured members by 1834, but the majority of the members, taking the lead from the speaker, were opposed to the new policies which were being dictated from London.

The year 1839 may be regarded as a turning point in the parliamentary life of the Bahamas because in the elections of that year Turks, Crooked and Acklin islands sent representatives to the House prepared to support official government policy in an Assembly which was equally divided between old reactionaries and new progressives. The government party included members of the British forces stationed in Nassau. In the climate of cooperation the new governor Sir F. Cockburn persuaded the House of Assembly to pass an amendment which changed payment of official salaries from a limited period of seven years to the duration of 'the whole reign of the Queen'. Nowhere else in the West Indies had there been found so conspicuous an example of confidence in the person of the young Queen. Two years later there came the implementation of another reform, separation of the functions of the Executive and Legislative Councils, the maximum membership of each being restricted to nine persons.

The first reference to education in the Bahamas occurs in 1721, when minutes of the Society for the Promotion of Christian Knowledge recorded a request for assistance from Mr Isaacs, 'the only schoolmaster in the Bahamas having a fee paying school for 20 pupils in his home in New Providence'. He was sent five pounds worth of religious books. Another school with a religious curriculum, Mr Flavell's, was operating by 1725 on Harbour Island. Governor Woodes Rogers established contact with the Society for the Propagation of the Gospel in Foreign Parts. They sent out a missionary in 1733. Despite legislation passed in 1735 to encourage education no school was opened until 1739, when a teacher paid by the SPG was recruited in Carolina.

In 1793 an American society, the Associates, opened a free charity school for Negro children which continued until 1844, when teachers and school were integrated with a school at Carmichael village. American Baptists and Methodists also started schools run by Negro missionaries during the decade 1790 to 1800.

The Methodists utilised white Bahamian teachers in their schools on New Providence, Harbour Island, Eleuthera and Abaco. By 1854 only one third of children were attending school in the Bahamas. Only 1,000, or half the total number, had begun the first stages of learning arithmetic.

In 1883 a special committee reported that only 6,000 pupils out of 10,000 were registered in settlements with over 25 children. About 2000 children within reach of schools did not attend. Thirty two large settlements had no schools, while there were only 24 Board schools as compared with 33 independent schools. Temporary prosperity during America's period of prohibition ironically led to the improvement of educational facilities in the Bahamas. Between 1919 and 1925 schools increased to 44, although only four were Board schools. So low, however, had the teaching profession fallen by 1930 that out of 60 regular teachers only three had school certificates and only 11 had passed the Cambridge Junior Examination.

By 1945 Board schools in Nassau were overcrowded and only seven institutions, mostly in New Providence, offered secondary education for the islands. In the Out islands there were then 63 Board schools, 43 grant-in-aid schools, 18 Anglican, 13 Roman Catholic and one Adventist. In 1950 a Training College was opened for 30 teachers in buildings on Oakes Field. It was closed in 1957.

Modern educational techniques in the Bahamas largely followed upon recommendations which were made in 1958 by Mr Houghton, Deputy Educational Adviser to the Secretary of State for the Colonies. These included the opening of a new Bahamas Teachers' College, a new Technical Institute, an Evening Institute, introduction of a sixth form at the Government High School, extension of the power of the Board and the establishment of an Advisory Council of Education. In 1964 the Bahamas affiliated with the University of the West Indies and in 1966 an office of the Department of Extra-Mural Studies was opened in the buildings of the Bahamas Teachers' Training College. In September 1968 the San Salvador Teachers' College was opened to provide academic and professional training for subordinate assistant and certified teachers on the Out islands. In recent years there has been considerable growth in the number of institutions, mostly operated by or in association with churches, catering to the needs of children under five years old. By 1971 New Providence had no less than 45 of these institutions, which were attended by between one third and one half of children aged between 3 and 4 years.

Administrations in the Bahamas have always been faced by the problems of communications. Separated by hundreds of miles of sea which are made dangerous by sand banks and protruding rocks and sometimes lashed by storms, the central government in Nassau for centuries had no effective methods of controlling what happened on the periphery of its scattered land areas. Reasons of distance alone would explain how it was possible for Guyanese middlemen to visit out islands of the Bahamas in 1838 and recruit negro men for work on their sugar plantations, without having to make arrangements for the families left behind. Distance too would account for the danger to Bahamian negro sailors who might be sold as slaves for American plantations when their boats were deliberately shipwrecked off the coasts of Florida. It was certainly distance from Nassau which encouraged the salt rakers on the Turks islands to seek independence from the government at Nassau.

Loss of Turks revenue in 1848, when the islands were put under the supervision of the Jamaican government, encouraged development of alternate wealth-producing activities within the remaining islands of the Bahamas. George Matthew, who governed the islands between 1844 and 1849, had done his best to lay solid foundations for the future. Despite the effect of a drought in 1844, Governor Matthew in four years secured a surplus revenue, reduced the public debt, enlarged the institutions dealing with the poor, established a hospital and dispensary service, provided a public library, placed the militia on a substantial basis, adjusted the civil list to suit the needs of the islands, readjusted tariff schedules and promoted fruit growing as a complementary economic activity to the working of salt ponds. Between 1842 and 1858 Bahama mails were carried between the islands and Britain by the Royal Mail Line, which used Nassau as a distributing centre for a few years until the land-locked harbour of Charlotte Amalie in the then Danish island of St Thomas was preferred as a transhipment for mail and passengers, and as a coaling and repair depot for ships. At the end of 1858 the decision was taken to switch Bahamian mails to the Cunard line, which took them via New York as an extension of the mail service recently begun between Great Britain and the United States.

Between 1830 and 1860 the forces which were transforming America built up to explosion point over slavery. But there was a greater dividing line between the people of the North and the people of the South. As a young South Carolinian said in 1860, 'We differ like Celt and Anglo-Saxon and there is no sufficient force in a "government of opinion" to keep us together against our will'. The differences were to end in what has been described as 'the bloodiest war that was fought in all the nine-teenth century'. The years of financial panic and severe depression which preceded the great American bloodletting hardly affected the South, which accordingly renewed its faith in cotton and strengthened a belief that direct trade with European firms could be maintained independently of the New York money market. Southerners before the outbreak of war did not regard war with the North as inevitable or that it would last long if it came. Some even believed that an independent South could revive the slave trade and through cheap labour assist in the economic develop-ment of Cuba, Santo Domingo, Mexico and central American territories. By 4 February 1861, six of the seven rebel common-wealths had formed a new Government of the Confederate States of America, with a new flag, the 'Stars and Bars'. Aggression by South Carolinians at Fort Sumter provoked Lincoln to call forth the militia of the several states of the Union and four days later to order the blockade of Confederate ports on April 19. General Gorgas Confederate Chief of Ordnance reported in August 1863 that freight steamers running between Wilmington in North Caro-lina and Bermuda brought in arms, steel, zinc and various other articles of war in large quantities. But the principal arsenal of the South was in the centre of one of the richest coal and iron regions of the new Republic. There was sympathy in Britain and France for the Confederates, whose independent status as a 'belligerent power' entitled them to the privilege of buying and taking away whatever they could pay for. Britain, however, resisted French pressure to intervene directly and in 1864 Lord Palmerston sent away a pro-southern delegation from England with the remark that

> *They who in quarrels interpose,*
> *Will often wipe a bloody nose.*

Nonetheless British ship builders began at an early date to provide Confederates with ships which were allowed to 'escape' from British waters to unpoliced ports where they were equipped with guns and munitions. The *Oreto*, which had been so allowed to escape from Liverpool to the Bahamas in March 1862, was, before her capture in 1864, to take no less than 40 Union merchantmen in prizes. About 18 of these 'escape' vessels so damaged Northern commerce at sea that marine insurance rates were raised 900 per cent.

If Bermuda was the source of war materials for the Confederates, as General Gorgas said, the port of Nassau was an all-purpose base for their traders and men of all nations with whom they did business. The long low coast of the southern states extended for over 3,500 miles and from a variety of ports vessels, heavily laden with confederate bales of cotton, risked the northern blockade to bring their wares to market in Nassau. The atmosphere of Nassau soon was exchanged from that of 'indolent acquiescence in its own obscurity', as G. J. H. Northcroft wrote in 1899 'for an air of importance and financial intoxication . . . Nassau became the principal base of supplies for the blockaded Atlantic ports'.

James Stark in his *History and Guide to the Bahamas* (1891) says that the first Confederate vessel arrived at Nassau from Charleston with 144 bales of cotton on 5 December 1861. By the end of the war 397 vessels had entered Nassau from Confederate ports, and 588, mostly steamers, had sailed for Southern ports. The usual time taken between Nassau and Charleston or Wilmington was 48 hours. According to Stark 22 steamers altogether were shipwrecked off Charleston and Wilmington and another 42 were captured by Unionists. The impact of these years, which have been called the 'golden age' of Nassau, is reflected in the rise of imports and exports between 1860 and 1864. In the year preceding the outbreak of war between the Confederate South and the Unionist North imports into Nassau were valued at £234,029 and exports at £157,350. In 1864 imports had risen to £5,346,112 and exports to £4,672,398.

Stark mentioned that in the two months of January and February 1865, no less than 20 steamers ran the blockade into Nassau, bringing 14,182 bales of cotton valued at $2¾ million. 'Ships', said Stark, 'were packed to the ceilings, streets were crowded with bales, boxes and barrels. Fortunes were made in a few weeks or months. Money was spent and scattered in the most extravagant and lavish manner. The town actually swarmed with Southern refugees, captains and crews of blockade runners. Every available space, in and out of doors was occupied. Men lay on verandahs, walls, docks and floors. Money was plentiful and sailors sometimes landed with $1500 in specie. Wages were doubled, liquors flowed freely and the common labourer had his champagne and rich food. Not since the days of the buccaneers and pirates had there been such times in the Bahamas.' According to Stark, blockade-running cheered the Southern heart because it was the connecting link between the Southern Confederacy and the outer world. The Bahamian treasury benefited from the golden age of spending and the legislature took the opportunity of the new prosperity to construct the Royal Victoria Hotel. It was built, says Stark, 'in the most elaborate and expensive manner . . . that the Nassau people might sumptuously entertain their Southern friends'. The war years, however, were not without hardships for the people of Nassau. During the period 1862 to 1864 there were outbreaks of yellow fever and the disease persisted until it was 'driven away' by the great hurricane of 1866, which was accompanied by a tidal wave that swept over Hog Island, laid Nassau low and caused failure of crops.

The golden days of Nassau, during which the government had been able to wipe off a public debt of £47,786 departed as soon as the American Civil War ended in April 1865. The expenditure on government had risen from £36,875 in 1860 to £79,366 in 1865 and the civil establishment of 200 salaried officers was far in excess of the capacity of a 'poor and diminutive colony to support'. The public debt had risen again to £31,153 by 1867. Nor were there guests for that 'splendid monument of legislative folly', the Royal Victoria Hotel, which within two years involved all who had anything to do with it 'in loss and embarrassment', despite its being rent free and aided by a steamer subsidised at costly rate.

In 1861 a select Committee of the House of Commons divided the British overseas dependencies (exclusive of India) into colonies proper: North America, South Africa, West Indies, Ceylon, Mauritius, New Zealand and the Australian colonies (except West Australia); and military garrisons, naval stations, convict depots and dependencies maintained chiefly for objects of imperial policy. In this second category were placed Malta, Gibraltar, the Ionian Islands, Hong Kong, Labuan, Bermuda, the Bahamas, St Helena, the Falklands, West Australia, Sierra Leone, Gambia and the Gold Coast. By that year the effects of free trade had come near to dissolving the British Empire. The West Indies alone had seen their exports drop from £6,415,765 in 1842 to £4 million in 1861, while their imports had increased by more than half a million pounds. To be valued as an 'object of imperial policy' might have appeared to the Bahamians at the time as more worthwhile than to be considered as a colony which was doomed sooner or later to obtain self-government, irrespective of its physical resources.

The first round of 'Bahamian versus Englishman' was to be more politico-religious than strictly secular. The See of Nassau had been formed in 1861 and the Church of England with 1600 members and the Presbyterian church with 150 were costing the government Treasury over £5000 per year, or a tax of 3s 5d per head on a population which comprised 3000 Wesleyans and 4000 Baptists who received no grants in aid. The financial embarrassment of the colony seemed reason enough to promote a policy of disendowment. But the movement also received strength from offended 'loyal Protestants', who rebelled against the introduction of 'semi-Romish' doctrines and practices of the High Church party. Great animosity was released during elections in 1868 when the 'church party' was said to have spent £1500; 'the ordinary price of votes' varying in some districts of New Providence 'from three to five dollars'. Governor Rawson seems to have displayed marked partiality by 'standing on the steps of his verandah', waving his handkerchief in honour of the six victorious members for New Providence. One of the promoters of disendowment that year records that the Union Jack was dipped twice in honour of the Anglican victory. 'And thus', he wrote, 'the flag which all parties and all classes, both white and black, both Dissenters and churchmen had looked up to with the profoundest sentiments of love and loyalty as the emblem of universal and impartial justice was basely prostituted in honour of a partisan triumph'. The Bahamian who did not want to subsidize High Church practices still wanted very much to live under the Union Jack. A year later the legislature enacted the Disestablishment Bill. The Anglican Church became autonomous in 1875, although nominally under allegiance to the Archbishop of Jamaica. The controversy over ritual persisted, however, and in the 1920s led Bishop Shedden to seek the aid of the secular Courts in order to uphold his spiritual jurisdiction. The Bahamas had come under the Catholic See of South Carolina in 1858, but no resident priest arrived until 1885. The modern growth of the Catholic Church within the islands really began with the opening of a priory in Dunmore House which the Benedictine Monastery of St John's acquired in 1893. The first bishop was installed on 5 July, 1960.

When the American Civil War ended Nassau's temporary boom, the residents of the islands fell back upon their normal occupations, raising crops and livestock, fishing, wrecking, salt-raking and sponging. A new agricultural project was started in 1884, when at the urging of Sir Henry Blake two or three plantations were put under sisal. The fibre-yielding agave, which took its name from the Port of Sisa in Yucatan, had been introduced by Colonial Secretary Rogers Nesbitt in 1845 and had been developed as a plantation crop by an Irish American Mr Howell. Little progress had been made, however, because of difficulties in decorticating, scarcity of investment funds, competition from other occupations like wrecking and finally the American Civil War. Three years after Sir Henry Blake had revived interest in its economic potential, another Governor Sir Ambrose Shea was able to attract large investment from Britain. No less a person than the great imperialist statesman Joseph Chamberlain formed a company and sent his son Neville, Britain's future Prime Minister, to take charge of a plantation and factory on Andros. Bahamians have blamed the failure of the Chamberlain enterprise on the legendary Chickcharnies of Andros, but the cultivation of sisal was undertaken with the highest hopes of success. The Governor told the Legislature in the opening ceremony of 1891, that the remarkable fibre product had been acknowledged to be the 'best of its kind in the British or American markets'.

The House of Assembly in reply to this address from the Head of Government announced proudly that the 'Colony has been lifted from a state of depression to one in which your Excellency well observes, we are steadily widening the solid basis of future independence'. The Legislature's remarks about independence were no doubt a pointed reference to the decision of the British government to withdraw Imperial troops from the Colony in that year. The confidence of the Bahamian governor and Legislature in the future of sisal was reflected by Dr Daniel Morris, then Assistant Director of the Royal Gardens at Kew, in a paper read before the Society of Arts in 1896. Dr Morris said that probably no part of the world, other than Yucatan, was so favourably situated for carrying on the sisal industry as the Bahama islands. He estimated that at the end of 1897 exports would reach about 6000 tons. But sisal never produced the hoped-for wealth which had been the dream of Ambrose Shea and Chamberlain. When fibre from the Bahamas was in demand during the Second World War £50,000 put up by the British government was allotted for growing Sanseviera on a number of Out-islands. Bahamians were not attracted to a crop which in its best year of 1902 had earned £37,574.

Disease put paid to the very profitable sponge industry of the Bahamas, which by 1901 gave employment to approximately one third of the working population and earned £152,000 for the islands in 1917. In 1938 the industry was wiped out by a fungoid. It is only gradually being revived. The significance of sponges for the Bahamian economy is best illustrated by comparison of the income brought from its sales abroad in 1917 (£152,000) with the total value of Bahamian export trade (slightly over £130,000) in 1889. One source of income, 'cannabis indica', seems not to have been generally exploited by the population. Yet the plant grew on the Bahamas, if we are to believe a letter printed in the *Troy Budget* of 8 March, 1887. It was written by the Hon. C. L. MacArthur, an early booster of tourism. He wrote: 'This leafy paradise should be enjoyed in a hammock swung from the banyan's branches . . . a delicious cigar will help to intensify the tropical felicity . . . if that don't do it the Cannabis indica grows within sight from what is derived the famous hasheesh which is the King of all narcotics in weaving a dreamy spell about its votaries . . . here's the spot where the drug can be easiest had '. Although cannabis may not have been grown for sale, tobacco had extensively been cultivated in the 'seventies and cigars were first exported in 1878.

Writing in 1902, when there were little more than 55,000 residents of the Bahamas, the Governor, Sir Gilbert Carter, complained that there was ' not one master carpenter, blacksmith or mason in the colony, and no means of training these and possible exponents of other industrial arts. . . . It is almost impossible in a Colony like this, where the revenue is never sufficient for the calls upon it, to make the radical charges which would be necessary in order to place this question upon the proper foundation, and unfortunately so far little disposition has been shown by the legislature to assist the government in its efforts to encourage practical agriculture, which, after all is the industry upon which the mass of the people must rely, and about which they at present know next to nothing.'

In that year Nassau had already been connected by cable to Florida and the place was becoming more desirable to live in, although many of 'its more active spirits' had emigrated to the United States. George Shattuck said that there was probably no cleaner or more wholesome town than Nassau, 'a village of picturesque houses and pretty gardens'. H. M. Flagler had recently renovated the Royal Victoria Hotel (where Lady Brassey was unable to get a meal in 1883), the Colonial had been built on the waterfront to accommodate 600 guests and Clifton House was neat and well managed. Sir Gilbert Carter and his American wife had also by this time embellished the gardens of Government House with native and imported plants. In every respect Nassau seemed set to grow and expand at the expense of the other islands of the Bahamian family. Any other development was unlikely, for as Sir Gilbert Carter noted in 1902: 'in the last Assembly not a single out-island constituency was able to send its own representative and it followed that the whole of the members were recruited from the islands of New Providence, which in itself sends 8 (out of 29) members to the Assembly'.

3 Modern Times

Telephones were introduced to Nassau in 1907, electricity supply in 1909 and wireless communications established with Florida in 1913. In 1908 the Royal Bank of Canada opened a branch in Nassau. Between 1897 and 1917 the New York and Cuba Mail Steamship Co. (Ward Line) ran regular mail services to Nassau. For over 30 years up to 1921, however, there was no direct steamer link with Great Britain, although the Scrutton line made calls at Nassau on the way to Belize (British Honduras). An indication of the slow-moving pace of life in the Bahamas in the first two decades of the twentieth century is to be found in the time it took to produce the King George v issue of stamps. King George v ascended the throne on 6 May 1910, but no series of stamps bearing his head went on sale in the Bahamas until 1912.

The outbreak of war caused some exchanges and movements in and out of the Bahamas. Nearly 700 Bahamians engaged in active war service while the islanders contributed over £47,000 to the Allied efforts. The economy relied mainly on tourism, sponge and sisal for most of the duration, but the islanders had to contend with a failure of the Bank of Nassau (1916) and severe shortages in 1917. As a relief measure, in 1918 labourers were recruited and sent to work in Charleston, South Carolina.

No House of Assembly met between 1910 and 1919, the year in which two American seaplanes flew from Miami as harbingers of the new era. The new Bahamian legislature had little to cheer about, with a prospect of unemployment for returning soldiers and labourers, falling world prices for their products and a public debt of £69,423. It looked as if the islands were about to pass through yet another period of hard times. But something was stirring on the American mainland, which would change the behaviour of American people for decades and scatter treasure once more around the Bahamas.

Prohibition throughout America arose from a combination of forces, the moral idealism of the Progressive era meeting the stresses engendered by war. The social upheavals caused by war, resentment against German brewers and the need to conserve materials used by distillers, helped prohibitionists to obtain *national* prohibition as a part of the Constitution. The Eighteenth Amendment passed Congress in December 1917, was approved in January 1919 and went into effect in January 1920. The Volstead Act of October 1919 had defined 'intoxicating liquor as any beverage containing over one half of 1 per cent of alcohol'. It supplemented the Prohibition amendment.

Illegal drink suddenly became an exciting adventure for millions of Americans and provided riches for gangsters, bootleggers, moonshiners, rum-runners, hijackers, racketeers, trigger men, venal judges, corrupt police, crooked politicians and operators of speakeasies. Gangsters created 'empires of vice', and corruption, the 'Tommy' gun and the 'poisoned cup' became trademarks of a new decadence in society. An American cynic of the thirties described the American dilemma as follows :—

> *Prohibition is an awful flop*
> *We like it*
> *It can't stop what it's meant to stop.*
> *We like it.*
> *It's left a trail of graft and slime*
> *It's filled our land with vice and crime*
> *It don't prohibit worth a dime,*
> *Nevertheless, we're for it.*

The financial cost of prohibition was considerable for the United States. A London newspaper in 1928 put it at £2,600,000 a year and reported that 3500 officials with 390 vessels and five seaplanes were engaged in operations against rum-runners. There was also loss of life. Over a six-year period, 49 officials were killed and 203 wounded. Not only rum was involved. It was estimated that 8000 tons of brandy and whisky were shipped monthly from English ports and that an average cargo was valued at £300,000. The battle for liquor was not one-sided, however. Over six years 839 boats were seized, and hijackers were active on seas, which were sometimes as destructive of bootleggers as

were Federal Agents. Nassau was a convenient place to transact
the business of illegal drink, and the revenues from official duties
on liquor reaching the port were attractive to an administration
urgently in need of funds. Customs receipts, which had stood at
£103,492 in 1919, reached £640,798 four years later. Money
became the god of all those who benefited from the Puritan
legislation against intoxicating liquors and bootlegging changed
all the social virtues which had slowly been emerging in Nassau.
'Rum', wrote Sir Etienne Dupuch in 1967, 'was now King. And
still is today'.

Another writer in 1934 put another side of the coin. Before
rum-running, he said, there were no restaurants, street lighting,
sewers or macadamised roads. Now churches were renovated,
charities supported, taxis replaced horse cabs, water ran in city
taps, real estate boomed, a casino opened and new hotels were
built. The first decade of illicit drinking in the States saw
modern tourism firmly established upon the islands. In
these years beach mansions and stately homes were erected
by rich Americans along Eastern Road, the Grove, Prospect
Ridge and Cable Beach. A beginning was made, too, to try
to attract visitors to Bimini and a small market began in the
buying and selling of the outer cays.

Major Bell, who wrote *Bahamas, Isles of June* in 1934, noted
that Canadian banks also made millions of dollars out of the
liquor trade. He said that American prohibition helped to establish a chain of Canadian branch banks all the way from Montreal
to Belize. He claimed too that the men who made the greatest
fortunes in Nassau never sailed a ship nor sold to any person
in the United States a pint of booze; buyers flooded their offices,
took liquor direct to chartered ships and sailed away. According
to Bell most of the liquor was American-made and had been shipped abroad for storage prior to prohibition, but had travelled by
way of Europe and the islands.

During the palmy days of prohibition a trial flight had been
made from Nassau to Miami on 9 October 1928 and on 2 January
1929. Pan American Airways put the Bahamas 'on the map' for
American visitors by inaugurating a scheduled winter service.
Exactly one year later the airline extended its flights in the winter to give a daily service.

The American mood was changing about prohibition and the Democrats called for its abandonment on their platforms in 1932. By December 1933 enough states had ratified the Twenty-First Amendment to repeal the Eighteenth. The control of liquor was returned to the states of which only seven maintained prohibition. By the 1950s not a single state banned totally the sale of beer, whisky or wine, although some states left localities the right to ban sales of alcoholic beverages within their jurisdictions.

Before the Americans developed a new tolerance for intoxicating alcohol their country had entered upon the period of the great depression, which opened with the panic on Wall Street of October 1929. Two years later Europe was feeling the effects and in September 1931 Great Britain was forced to abandon the gold standard. When Roosevelt took office in 1933 the banking system of the United States was on the verge of collapse and there were almost 12 million unemployed on the brink of starvation! In his second inaugural address of January 1937 Roosevelt still could speak of 'ten millions of citizens who at this very moment are denied the greater part of what the very lowest standards of today call the necessities of life'. He saw 'millions of families trying to live on incomes so meagre that the pall of family disaster hangs over them day by day'. He saw 'one third of a nation ill-housed, ill-clad, ill-nourished'.

By comparison, what might be said of the Bahamas in these years of hard times which were also hitting its powerful neighbour and its responsible Mother Country beyond the seas? Not everything was stagnant, for in 1933 a new company, Bahamas Airways Ltd., started operations to provide mail and passenger facilities between New Providence and some of the Out-islands. This company was incorporated in 1936, when it operated four aircraft making monthly flights from Nassau to Cat Cay and Bimini, fortnightly to Marsh Harbour, Hope Town, Green Turtle Cay and West End, and weekly to Harbour Island, Spanish Wells, Governor's Harbour and Rock Sound. A further service connected Nassau to Miami and West Palm Beach.

In 1949 British South American Airways, which had begun to stop at Nassau two years earlier on its way between London and Santiago, bought out Bahamas Airways. Later in the year, when BOAC took over British South American Airways, Bahamas

Airways became a wholly-owned BOAC subsidiary. In April 1959 BOAC sold 80 per cent of its shares to Skyway Bahamas Holding Company, but bought them back again in December 1960. BOAC's control of Bahamas Airways was maintained throughout most of the 'sixties until in October 1968 John Swire and Sons Ltd., the owners of Cathay Pacific, bought 85 per cent of BOAC's holdings in Bahamas Airways. BOAC maintained its association with the Bahamas airline until it went into voluntary liquidation in October 1970.

A chance meeting between Bahamian real estate agent Sir Harold Christie and Sir Harry Oakes at Palm Beach led to the arrival in the Bahamas during 1934 of the Canadian multi-millionaire, who built Oakes Field, refurbished the old Colonial Hotel as the British Colonial Hotel and developed much of the 7000-acre property he had bought south-west of Nassau. Like other overseas investors whose money circulated quickly to provide employment Harry Oakes was welcomed in Nassau. In 1938 he was elected to the House of Assembly and later was nominated to the Legislative Council. Oakes' money and his modernisation of the British Colonial hotel helped to give employment to approximately 1500 Bahamians and was very timely because the sponge industry collapsed in 1939. Tourism had been steadily advancing through these difficult years and helped to sustain an economy which could not be entirely isolated from the effects of the great American and European depressions. There had been a major change of United States attitude to the Americas following a goodwill tour of Latin America by President-elect Hoover in 1928. At his inaugural address, Hoover said: 'We have no desire for territorial expansion, for economic or other domination of other people'. In 1930 the Reuben Clark memorandum repudiated the Roosevelt Corollary of the Monroe Doctrine by emphasising that the Monroe doctrine 'states a case of the United States vs Europe and not the United States vs Latin America'. At the Montevideo Conference of American States Secretary Hull approved a pact asserting that 'no state has the right to intervene in the internal or external affairs of another'. By an agreement in 1939 the United States gave up its rights to intervene in Panama and increased its annual payments for canal rights. A year before the State Department added a Division of Cultural

10 *A beach on Stocking Island, Exuma*

11 *Man O' War Cay, Abaco*

Relations. All these changes of political manoeuvre were to help the Allies when America joined the Second World War in 1941.

The first indication of a movement away from a policy of isolation was made by President Roosevelt in his 'quarantine' speech in Chicago on 5 October 1937. 'We are determined to keep out of war', he said, '. . . but we cannot have complete protection in a world of disorder in which confidence and security have broken down'. Much later on 3 November 1939, after the Second World War had started, Congress repealed an arms embargo so that arms could be sold to the Allies. In September 1940 Roosevelt announced the transfer to Great Britain of 50 over-age destroyers. In return Britain gave the United States sites for naval bases on Newfoundland and Bermuda and rent-free leases for six sites in the Caribbean and South Atlantic. The Bahamas was one of the six sites selected and from this controversial action of Roosevelt's was to come the dynamic thrust which was to pull the neglected Bahamas firmly into a modern American expansionist orbit. Improved communications made possible the realisation by millions of Americans of vacations in the sunshine islands near their coasts. The boom in building realised by the American creation of a naval base at George Town, Exuma and an air base at Oakes Field, took the Bahamian economy across a hump of inequality which foretold the end of colonial wage rates and the beginning of the search for an equation with American labour remuneration.

Two people were killed and 25 injured in riots against unequal pay which occurred on the Oakes Field project in 1942.

On 7 July 1942 occurred the unsolved murder of Sir Harry Oakes. The reason for the killing, many Bahamians believe, stemmed from Oakes' resistance to proposals for the operation of casinos in the Bahamas. The Duke of Windsor's personal intervention in this case was severely criticised at the time and does not appear to have been supported by the Colonial Office.

Despite these two regrettable occurrences, riot and murder and a very large fire, Nassau achieved a new importance during the war as an RAF training centre, as a halt for the trans-Atlantic ferry service and as a base for ocean patrol and air sea rescue work which was part of the anti-submarine campaign in the Caribbean

12 *(opposite) Bimini Islands, from the air*

E

and Atlantic. The members of the Select Committee of the House of Commons had seemingly been justified when in 1861 they had appreciated the role that the Bahamas might play in imperial policy.

The Japanese attack on Pearl Harbour in the afternoon of 7 December 1941 led the United States Congress to declare war first against Japan and a few days later against Germany and Italy. The American action soon cut the supply of visitors who fell from 14,741 in 1941 to 3,639 in 1943. The government of the Bahamas would have been very hard pressed to find alternative sources of employment had there not been a brisk demand for labour on the American bases. A high level of employment at the bases was maintained until 1943. Bahamian workers were also sent on contracts to the United States. Approximately £200,000 was later remitted by them to their families in the islands. Between 1921 and 1943 the population on New Providence had grown by 20,375, or nearly two and a half times its size in 1921. Led by the Duke of Windsor, the government appointed an Out Island Economic Investigating Committee to propose methods of improvement of harbours, roads, provision of inter-island ships, development of air transportation, public works programmes and the raising of Out island levels to those on New Providence. Further economic growth arose from exports of fish (worth £75,425, in 1943), a temporary salt boom on Inagua (£34,489 in 1941) and the phenomenal advance of shell and straw work (£177,161, in 1943). By the beginning of 1944 over 1000 Bahamians were still on the payroll of the RAF and US forces.

Canning and freezing of fish had also been established at West End on Grand Bahama in 1940, when General Sea Foods employed just under 200 persons. Despite appearances of prosperity and a government expenditure of over £1 million for the year ending in November 1943, health and housing lagged far behind other improvements.

A cost of living increase of 89 per cent over a 4-year period had resulted in generally inadequate diets and a high incidence of tuberculosis. The Economic Adviser to the government, Professor Henry Richardson, had no hesitation in recommending a 'carefully graduated system of income tax' and asserted that 'there would be greater advantages if greater responsiblity for certain local affairs could be undertaken by representative local councils'.

Farming, he noted was handicapped by insecurity of tenure, soil impoverishment, lack of rotation of crops and absence of measures to counter soil erosion. Farmers, he said, required a minimum of 5-8 acres for profitable undertakings and there was place for large-scale projects, requiring considerable capital and technical management. The adviser also recommended the improved marketing of all agricultural produce and suggested that animals should be slaughtered on the Out islands before despatch to Nassau in refrigerated ships.

In an attempt to encourage men to go back to farming on the Out islands the British government in 1943 also provided a grant of £50,000 which would give employment to 1370 persons working at three-monthly intervals on the planting of Sanseviera on Cat Island, Long Island, Abaco, Andros and Exuma. The attempt was justified, if only to try and persuade Bahamians to go back to the land, from which the war and alternative highly paid employment elsewhere had drawn them. So great had been the drift that fishing as an industry had suffered and many Bahamians had grown accustomed to living off imported foods.

The importance of local food production and the expansion of fisheries within the Caribbean had received priority of attention at the first West Indian Conference, which the Anglo-American Caribbean Commission had promoted in 1944. The Bahamas had been represented at this meeting in Barbados and also took part in the second conference at Charlotte Amalie in 1946. But the Bahamas did not participate in the wider political conference, which was held at Montego Bay in 1947 to study closer unity of the British Caribbean. As a consequence the Bahamas moved farther and farther away from the liberalising political developments which were changing the whole concept of future relationships for the region and followed paths which seemed to their oligarchs to promise much more than they might gain from association with a diversity of distant islands. The Bahamas were not, it was decided, part of the West Indies. Their future could be better fashioned by their own legislature of businessmen, who by continuous production of wealth would be able to satisfy the increasing demands of the Bahamian people for a better life. Tourism was a natural base for such economic advancement and in the early 'fifties visitors to the Bahamas had reached 68,502 in a single year. It was not, however, until after Castro's takeover of Cuba in 1959 that the golden hordes of tourists began to arrive. By 1968 they had reached 1,072,213. The impact of economic growth was reflected in the resident population figures of New Providence and Grand Bahama for the years between 1953 and 1970. On New Providence the figures rose from 46,125 in 1953 to 80,907 in 1963 and to 101,182 in 1970. On Grand Bahama they rose from 4095 in 1953 to 9093 in 1963 and to 26,073 in 1970. Concurrently with expanded tourist development there had been continuous growth in residential complexes, US Naval facilities and industrial and agricultural projects. Money attracts money and in the 'sixties, following hard upon the imaginative creation of Freeport, which had been made possible by the Hawksbill Creek Act, the Bahamas became a centre for multi-million Euro-dollar trade. By 1971 nearly 200 banks had been licensed. Almost complete freedom from direct taxation also attracted thousands of companies from the United Kingdom, the United States and Canada to register local offices. The Bahamas, besides being tourist havens, now had become internationally recognised as capitalist paradises.

But other factors were at work besides those released by the business oligarchs and their collaborators. The leaven of political action had started among the representatives of the black Bahamian people who wanted not only higher wages but opportunities to enjoy the rights of equal citizenship in the lands of their birth. A mulatto member of the House of Assembly, Mr William Cartwright, started the ball rolling by forming a nucleus from which the Progressive Liberal Party was to emerge in 1955. Soon after its formation this party was joined by Lynden O. Pindling, the London-educated lawyer who became first Prime Minister of the Bahamas on 10 July 1973. The PLP from the beginning appealed to the fundamentalist, scripture-reading Bahamian with a slogan 'all the way' taken from the Old Testament text which admonishes: 'And Thou shalt remember all the way which the Lord Thy God has led thee'. For the ordinary black Bahamian anxious to have a full share in the prosperity that was spreading slowly to some black Bahamians, the old guard of Bay Street business boys represented Egypt's Pharaoh. They saw in Lynden Pindling a leader to their promised land. The anti-discrimination bill of Sir Etienne Dupuch in 1956 greatly encouraged many to walk tall in their homelands, but there was still a long trek ahead. The PLP showed their growing strength when they supported the Taxicab Union strike of 1958 and obtained promises of constitutional changes from the British Secretary of State, including 'universal adult suffrage'. The Bahamas House of Assembly refused to pass the reforms which were recommended subsequently by the Secretary of State, but women were given the vote in 1962 by an act of 1961, the same year in which the PLP announced its intention to overthrow 'the Bay Street Boys'. The PLP did not come to power in 1962 but gained a majority of votes (32,299 as compared with the UBP's 26,826). In 1963, at a constitutional conference held in London and attended by leaders of the two major political parties, the Colonial Office agreed to the introduction of internal self-government in the Bahamas. The legislature was to comprise a Senate of 15 while the House of Assembly would have 33 members until 1967, when they would be increased to 38. In the elections of 1967 the United Bahamian Party won 18 seats, the PLP 18, Labour one, and there was one independent. Lynden Pindling was invited to form a government. When the next General Election was held on 10 April 1968 the PLP won 29 seats and the UBP seven. Labour and independents shared the remaining two seats. Further constitutional changes were made effective on 10 May 1969 when Ministers were granted almost all but complete independence from Westminster. The PLP won 29 seats in the general election of 1972, which was fought on a platform of early independence. The Free National Movement, which had been reconstructed from elements of the UBP, won 9 seats. In the presence of the Prince of Wales the Bahamas became independent on 10 July 1973.

The first of the Indies to be discovered by the men of the Old World, the Bahamas lie on the doorsteps of the most powerful nation in the New World. Its ability to survive as an independent entity in a world of increasing interdependence seems as assured as that of any other country. There is plenty of goodwill towards the islanders by governments and people of the friendly North American neighbouring states of Canada and America, while Britain and the former British Caribbean countries are no less eager to assist in ways within their capacities whenever invited to do so. There are also signs that government and investors have been drawing closer together in their objectives to build a better Bahamas.

With so much goodwill, the real difficulties of the Bahamas have as much if not more chance of being successfully tackled as those to be found elsewhere in today's world of ever-increasing problems. In their solution a considerable contribution will be made by the more than two million visitors who are expected to visit the islands yearly by 1980.

II FOREGROUND

4 The Biminis, Berries and Andros

Two Spanish words *bajo* (meaning shallow) and *mar* (meaning sea) have combined to form *bahama*. This arrangement of the two words appeared in a map of 1523 to describe one of the larger islands and since then has gradually been used of the little and great Bahama banks, the Great Bahama island and the entire archipelago of approximately 3000 islands, cays, rocks and sand-bores which are owned by the Commonwealth of the Bahamas islands. Some of the islands had been inhabited by members of the Indian tribes whom the Spaniards called los Lucaios, which was their translation of Lukku-cairi or 'island people', the simple title by which the Arawak Indians of the Bahamas were known. As late as 1670 when Charles II made a grant of the archipelago to the Lords Proprietors of the Carolinas the descriptive title 'islands of the Lucayans' was still being used as an alternative to Bahama islands'. The word Lucaya has survived into the present day on the Great or Grand Bahama island where the flourishing holiday resort of Lucaya is located only nine miles to the east of Freeport by Bell channel bay. The word is widely used to describe other Bahamian places and products.

The islands of the Bahamas extend along the north-east margin of the West Indies from the Straits of Florida to the eastern shores of Haiti. They have a total area of 5380 square miles of land scattered irregularly in large and small clusters between latitudes 20° 56' and 27° 25' N and longitudes 71° 10' and 79° 20' W. Four of the island groups, Andros and cays (2300), the Abacos and cays (649), the Inaguas (599) and Grand Bahama and cays (530) account for 4078 square miles, or over three quarters of the total land surfaces of the Commonwealth.

Population density in the Bahamas is however highest upon the small 21 x 7 mile island of New Providence, where over 60 per cent of Bahamian people live in a density of nearly 1300 to the square mile. Such a congregation of people on New Providence and its satellite Paradise island is remarkable when one considers that altogether the Bahamas occupy a region nearly as extensive as that of Great Britain. If superimposed upon a map of the United States, the Bahamas would cover an area from New York southwards to Atlanta and, in the widest part, westward from Cape Hatteras to New Bern in the Allegheny mountains of West Virginia!

The islands of the Bahamas are mostly composed of debris thrown up by corals and other calcareous organisms. They stand upon a shallow submerged platform separated by deep submarine troughs from the land areas of North America and the West Indies. This platform rises on all sides abruptly from the depth of the Atlantic Ocean. Its steepest ascent is along the eastern face where from a distance of 2500 fathoms at the bottom of the Atlantic the rise is completed in a little less than 35 miles.

The northwestern half of the platform contains the Great and Little Bahama Banks and carries the islands of Andros, the Berries, Biminis, Grand Bahama and the Abacos. It is shallower and less broken than the south eastern half where the islands are arranged in small groups, rise rapidly on all sides from a lower portion of the platform, and are separated from each other by wide passages. In the north-eastern portion of the Bahamas platform the Providence Channels and the 'bays' known as 'Tongue of the Ocean' and 'Exuma Sound' cut the Great Bahama Bank in the shape of an S and permit deep water from the Atlantic to enter inside the platform's centre. In the south-eastern portion of the platform which extends down to the Caicos and Turk islands erosion by waves has destroyed whatever banks might have once existed and the Atlantic can flow freely through passages between the islands.

The Biminis, North and South, are the most northerly parts of a small chain of islands, cays and reefs which lie upon the western side of the northwestern tip of the Great Bahama Bank. Yachtsmen crossing the Gulf Stream from Miami usually set a course for Gun Cay Light 43 miles distant. The journey in an average cruiser making a speed of ten knots can be done within 5 hours.

North Bimini harbour where seaplanes land hourly from Miami during the days of the high winter season is only minutes away by air. Aeroplanes from Nassau and South Florida land daily throughout the year on South Bimini where the Bahamian government maintains a runway extending to 5000 feet. The two Biminis are connected by ferry boat. The Biminis are frequently referred to in the single form as Bimini, although they are separated by water from each other. North Bimini is only seven miles long and is very narrow and flat, the highest elevation being less than 20 feet above sea level.

Bimini and fishing have almost been synonyms since the Compleat Angler Hotel first opened its doors in 1936. This is the hotel where Ernest Hemingway stayed. It is still popular with fishermen. Most of the accommodations and facilities on North Bimini are in Alice Town, which lies at the southern end of the island. There live most of the more than 1500 residents. Bimini's Blue Water Marina, owned by William Knight of Toledo, Ohio, was formerly known as the Compleat Angler Marina. It can accommodate and provision up to 32 yachts and can also supply fresh water, an essential item for yachtsmen but not always easy to obtain on Bimini, where it has been sold for as much as 20 cents a gallon.

Flanking the docks on North Bimini are fish pens maintained since 1948 by the Lerner Marine Laboratory, a field station of the American Museum of Natural History. The best time to visit is at feeding times, usually in the morning, between ten and eleven, and in the afternoon at four. Two popular eating places in Alice Town are Anchors Aweigh and the Red Lion.

South Bimini alone has laid claim to have the fabled spring which Ponce de Leon set out to find in 1512. One guide book has identified it as a spring several hundred yards up the coast from the Sunshine Inn, while another says it is covered in underbrush and difficult to find. Ponce de Leon certainly found it so. He was a Spaniard who rose from Court page to become governor in turn of East Hispaniola and of Puerto Rico. Towards the end of 1512, after an illness, he set out from Puerto Rico to seek the fountain which might restore his youthful vitality. According to popular reports of the time, the fountain was located on an island of the Bimini chain. According to a contemporary writer the fountain was a continual spring of running water of such marvellous virtue that the 'water thereof being drunk, perhaps with some diet, maketh old men young again'. Ponce de Leon was 52 when he started on his voyage. He lived for nine more years and died from a wound caused by a poisoned arrow, while living in retirement on Cuba. Would he have lived longer if he had drunk of the fountain of perpetual youth? Perhaps, but he never did find it, missing Bimini altogether, and landing instead on Florida, at a point a little to the north of where St Augustine now stands. His landfall was on Palm Sunday of the year 1513.

In this century Bimini has been much publicised in connection with another legend. According to some persons, a submerged 'stone wall' about 1800 feet long, discovered some years ago at a distance of 500 yards from North Bimini, is part of the lost continent of Atlantis. There have also been reports of the finding of an 'ancient temple'. Because these tales have a wide circulation I was not at all surprised to hear an American woman on Exuma say with the greatest conviction that she believed Bimini to be not only the site of the lost continent of Atlantis, but also the 'very cradle of human civilisation'. According to a popular guidebook printed in the United States a prediction that part of the lost continent of Atlantis would rise from the sea near Bimini was first made by a 'sleeping prophet' in 1923. Ten years later this same man made another prediction that temples from ancient Atlantis must be discovered at some time in the future near Bimini. Whatever interpretations may finally be put upon the new discoveries which link modern Bimini with legends of long ago some divers on Bimini have not been slow to make the most of new opportunities for gain.

When tongues grow tired of telling this tale, and other wonderfully true tales of fish which never got away, there is a handy topic of conversation to fall back on. It is the story of the floating whisky or gambling ship which ran aground off South Bimini in the days when prohibition in the United States had encouraged 'rum runners' to use Bahamian islands as places from which to launch illegal shipments of liquor to the mainland. This ship, wrecked in the 'twenties, suffered further sea changes during World War II when it was used by American pilots as a handy target for aerial bombing practice. Enough of its hulk still remains to allow its billing in modern tourist brochures as a place to explore and photograph. Other attractive areas for exploration by skin divers in the neighbourhood of the Biminis are the Victory Cays and Underwater Forest, the Turtle Rocks and Gun Cay near which 'man-made' structures have been seen.

The World Record chart of 1972 reported 24 record fish catches for Bimini since 1936. Among the fish found all the year round near Bimini and other islands of the Bahamas are barracudas, bonefish, grouper and tarpon. The Allison or yellow fin tuna may also be seen throughout the year but is most prevalent in the months of June, July and August in all deep water areas. The blackfin tuna or oceanic bonito are most common between May and September, while the blackfin 'giant' tuna, which sometimes weigh more than 1000 pounds, pass across the western banks of the Bahamas from early May until the middle of June. The best months for blue marlin are June and July. Sail fish are hunted in summer and autumn, while the heavy white marlin is sought in winter and spring.

The Ministry of Tourism sponsors two fishing tournaments every year: one from January to April, and the other from mid-June to mid-September. On Bimini five tournaments and a bonefish week are held each year.

Twelve miles to the south of Bimini on the privately owned island of Cat Cay an annual tournament is sponsored by the Cat Cay Club in May. Founded by Louis R. Wasey of New York in 1931, this club once had a reputation as an exclusive haven for the very rich. It later became inactive for some years, but was reopened in 1968 under new ownership. South Cat Cay nearby is also privately owned.

In recent years an artificial island called Ocean Cay nine miles south of Cat Cay has been thrown up by dredgers of aragonite sand working for Ocean Industries. The new land is expected to grow to about 200 acres before mining ceases.

Fishing and skin diving have transformed the economy of the Biminis in recent decades. Population, which numbered only 718 persons in 1943, had more than doubled 30 years later. In 1970 an announcement was made of a joint Bahamian-North American project which would give Bimini a harbour deep enough to accommodate cruise ships calling there from

Miami. This project also proposed 're-creation' of an old Bahamian town and building of an underwater futuristic city and undersea restaurant at a cost of several million dollars. However ambitious such plans might seem for a 1900-acre island with just a few palm-lined beaches it clearly demonstrates that with new thinking change is possible anywhere. It was new thinking which first made Bimini internationally famous, helped perhaps by Hemingway's *The Old Man and the Sea*. No one could have predicted such a change in the 'twenties when North Bimini was casually dismissed with a few lines in a Bahamian guidebook which was content to give the occupation of 610 islanders as 'wrecking: now sponging, fishing and growing sisal, coconuts and corn'.

The Berry Islands are stirrup-shaped clusters of islands anchored around the north-eastern edge of the Great Bahama Bank between 25° 22' and 25° 50' N. From the most northerly, Great Stirrup Cay in the Northwest Providence Channel, they extend for 40 miles in a general southerly direction to meet the waters of the Tongue of the Ocean as they flow outwards past the southeastern tip of Andros. Several harbours and other places to anchor are available for anyone who sails along their numerous cays, of which 30 may be described as large. A lighthouse on Great Stirrup Cay guards the south side of the Northwest Providence Channel, but its white light is secondary to that of the red lamp which flashes from the 200 ft tower of the United States Tracking Station. This red light may be seen by boats 18 miles from land. Over on the north coast of Great Stirrup Cay is Bertram Cove. The name commemorates Commander Bertram, a former captain of a British survey ship, HMS TWEED. He is buried there. Little Stirrup Cay, which lies slightly to the southwest of Great Stirrup Cay, is privately owned. It is low and rocky and has two ponds in the centre. Plans have been announced by its Texan owners for its development as a tourist resort.

The biggest development which has so far occurred in the Berry chain of islands has taken place on the largest of them, Great Harbour Cay. By October 1972 a multiple resort complex comprising a $2.7 million clubhouse, a 21,000 ft golf course, 76 villas,

40 waterfront houses, a well-equipped marina and sailing club had been established near Bullocks harbour. The 18-hole golf course was designed by Joe Lee, who had previously laid out the Disney World Course. It is kept green by the sprinkling of 200 million gallons of water each year. There is no shortage of fresh drinking water in the Berries. Tamboo Marina, adjacent to Bullocks Harbour, has been called the most elaborate in the western hemisphere. It has accommodation for 85 yachts up to 130 feet in length and gives round-the-clock service. Although it is off the beaten track Great Harbour Cay's airstrip (4,200 feet) brings it within 45 minutes flying time of Miami. Flying time between the islands and Nassau is 25 minutes. The census for 1970 put the total resident population of the Berries, at 443. It has attracted new settlers since. A third airstrip has been built on Cistern Cay to accommodate visitors to Cistern and Lignum Vitae Cays, two satellites of Great Harbour Cay, which like Little Stirrup Cay are also being developed.

Right in the centre of the Berries, Little Harbour Cay is a place of green hills and coconut groves. It is one of the prettiest of the Berries. Not far from Little Harbour going south are the Frozen and Alder Cays, both owned by Mr Willard F. Rockwell of Pittsburgh. These islands are beloved of birds, especially terns and brown noddies who nest in the rocks of the bluffs.

Bond's Cay, to the south of Alder, is also privately owned. Some miles to the south-west on Whale Cay a small island owned by Mr Wallace Groves, there is a well-kept aviary. Flamingos, peacocks, pheasants, geese, ducks and many other birds enjoy the hospitality of a man who has enhanced the natural beauty of the island by introducing the skills of modern landscape artists. Mr Wallace Groves, who also has a home in southwest England, is renowned as The Founder of Freeport on Grand Bahama. The larger island of Whale Cay immediately to the south of Little Whale is also privately owned. Bird Cay, which lies due west of Whale Cay, is owned by the proprietor of Bond's Cay. It is a highly developed settlement, well provided with modern amenities.

Chub Cay, which is not very far from the Joulters Cays that lie immediately to the north of Andros, is at the end of the Berry Chain. Its Crown Colony Club is the centre of a development

which includes an airstrip, marina, and residential accommodations. The airstrip is 5000 feet long and the landlocked harbour
can accommodate up to 65 boats.

Andros. It is only 15 miles by sea from the marina at Chub Bay
to Morgan's Bluff at the north-east end of the island of Andros.
This very large island of 2300 square miles is slowly emerging
from a long past of mystery and neglect. It is composed of three
separate land areas of which the north is the most highly developed. The middle contains the greatest percentage of water,
and the south is still in the early stages of development. Three
significant happenings since the First World War have helped
Andros to shift the emphasis of being a legendary land of elves,
remote Indian tribes, dense forests and primeval swamplands. The
most significant was the purchase of 35 miles of beach in the
Andros Town area by Dr Axel Wenner-Gren, the Swedish indus-
trialist. His Andros Yacht Club, built to the south of Fresh Creek,
and his Lighthouse Club advertised the magnificent tourist potential of an island with 100 miles of east coast facing upon the
largest barrier reef in the western hemisphere. Dr Wenner-Gren
was also responsible for clearing 4000 acres of farmland at Twin
Lakes and building an airstrip there 16 miles inland.

The choice of a site, one and a half miles from Fresh Creek as
headquarters for the Atlantic Undersea and Evaluation Test
Centre, was also to have major long-term significance. The headquarters of this organisation, commonly called AUTEC, moved
there in 1966 from Orlando, Florida. Andros' economy has since
obtained each year injections of about half a million dollars,
while over one hundred Bahamians still find employment at the
Centre.

The third important happening has been the construction of
roads which have followed upon the activities of lumber felling
for the manufacture of pulpwood. Andros was selected by a
British Land Resources survey team as one of the most suitable
islands for general agricultural expansion and in North Andros a
$10 million cattle breeding experiment may have great signifi-
cance for a Bahamian livestock industry. The optimistic attitudes
which are shown towards Andros throughout the Bahamas today

13 *Cotton Bay Golf Course, Eleuthera*
14 *Lighthouse Club, Fresh Creek, Andros*

contrast strangely with the defeatist note which was sounded in an official review of Bahamian Economic Conditions in 1944.

Now age-old attitudes have changed and Andros is the 'awakening giant'. Naval personnel at the Centre, after years of exploration along the depths of the Tongue of the Ocean, have been able to scotch the legend of the Lusca, the 'sea-monster' which generations of sea-faring Bahamians have accused of sucking boats and sailors into the maws of the blue holes round the coasts. Knowledge of these 'bottomless pits' has been greatly increased through the investigations of Dr George Benjamin, who in 1971 won the award of US diver of the year. Assisted by his sons, Peter and George, Dr Benjamin in 1967 discovered a cavern filled with stalactites and stalagmites 1200 feet below the level of the sea in a blue hole of the South Bight of Andros. Three years later Jacques Costeau made a film about the Benjamin Bluehole.

Scientific investigation of the Tongue of the Ocean has led to the speculation that oil may some day be discovered around Andros. The economic potential of vast stores of aragonite which build up underwater dunes around North and South Andros has already been appreciated. The right to exploit them commercially is held by Ocean Industries, the company which has been selling about two million tons of aragonite annually from Bimini deposits and which has rights as well over other deposits around the west coast of Eleuthera. The calcium carbonate which is the chief ingredient of aragonite is widely used in the manufacture of glass, lime, soft drinks and cement and even for the creation of artificial beaches on lands less bountifully supplied with sand than the Bahamas.

The growth of Andros since 1946 may perhaps best be charted in the rise of board schools from eight that year to 17 in 1960. Ten years later there were 21 schools on Andros, stretching from Red Bay, at the northwestern tip eastwards along the settlements of the East coast to Mars Bay near the southernmost point of Andros. There are no schools and no settlements on the west coast except at Red Bay in the extreme north of the island. Much of the coastal lands of West Andros is either marsh or completely under water. The creek mouths are prized by fishermen who enter them in search of tarpon. For several years the Mud, west

15 (opposite) Christchurch Cathedral, Nassau

F

of Andros, along the Great Bahamas Bank was the largest sponge fishing ground in the region.

A great variety of birds are found on the island which is densely covered with forests of pine, madeira, lignum vitae, mahogany and other woods. Among the birds are buzzards which are protected as 'scavengers', ducks, pigeons, doves, pelicans and parrots. Insects abound everywhere and the winged ones are adepts at discovering the taste of new blood.

Official brochures mention but make no strong claims for the existence of the 'chickcharnies' of Andros, who are supposed to be little pixies, red-eyed men with three fingers and toes who, when they are not up to their elvish tricks 'hang by their tails from cottonwood trees'. The inhabitants of Red Bay village, a remote township in the island, are sometimes described as descendants of Seminoles who landed there about the middle of the nineteenth century. It is certain that when a new road was opened some years ago, the people of Red Bay village were then living together as a single tribe ruled by a chief.

Despite the speeding tempo of the rhythm which has awakened the giant from centuries of deep slumber, Andros in 1973 had a population of no more than 9000.

Nearly 350 years after the Bahamas islands were discovered by Columbus, the numbers of people settled on Andros did not exceed 500, and in 1773 the entire population of the Bahamas had just reached 4000. People from other islands did not put down effective roots on Andros until 1780 and the island could not be described as 'settled' in any way until 1788, when 88 Loyalists and 254 negro slaves from the southern states of America and 16 immigrants from other islands of the Bahamas began serious cultivation of cotton on its northern shores. Until 1870 the northern parts of Andros were the places preferred by the majority of immigrants who had formed communities at Staniard Creek, Nicholls Town and Mastic Point. Only late in the nineteenth century were Exuman and Long Island immigrants prepared to cross one hundred miles of sea and settle upon virgin lands at South Andros. The population of Andros had increased notably by 1881 when there were 3434 residents. Sponge fishing, and the cultivation of sisal and other agricultural developments attracted still more people, so that the population reached 7545

by 1911. During the years of the First World War the sponge industry reached a peak with exports valued at £152,000. A decline
began with a series of hurricanes which destroyed many
beds and worse followed with the disastrous blight disease of
1938. Three years later men who had lived from sponge fishing
for decades had to accept seasonal jobs as field workers upon
farms in the Southern United States. This substitute source of
employment increased until in 1945 about 1000 workers, of
whom no less than 31 per cent went from South Andros, were
recorded as temporarily absent from their homes.

The Spanish name for Andros was the island of the Holy Spirit
and, if there is truth in the tradition that the Holy Spirit broods
over waters, there was good reason for the Spanish choice of
description. Water is particularly prevalent in the middle segments of Andros, where a series of three bights, called North,
Middle and South, separate the larger northern land area of Andros from Mangrove Cay and South Andros. The three channels of
water in these bights range in width from 5 to 25 miles and are
dotted by a multiplicity of small islands. The islands of the North
and Middle Bights are popular with hunters and fishermen.

The barrier reef which runs parallel to the east coast of Andros
is over 120 miles long and has few places of entry that are not
obstructed by an inner reef. The *Yachtsman's Guide to the
Bahamas* illustrates the entrances which are generally considered
to be safest. The cays to the north of Andros, Joulters, Candle and
Long are considered by those fishermen who have visited them as
ideal hunting grounds for bonefish (on the flats), tarpon, barracuda and mutton fish. Fresh water is available from wells on
South Joulter. The cays are uninhabited and the waters around
them reflect many textures of colour which change with the
lights from the sky. Nicholl's Town is headquarters for the Commissioner who is responsible for the Berries as well as the northern region of Andros. It has a resident population of 600 persons.
The dock of Andros Beach hotel at the northern tip of Nicholl's
Town is an official port of entry for ships. The Andros Beach
hotel is a cottage-villa resort landscaped over 300 acres close to
a mile-long beach. There are daily flights from Nassau to San
Andros. The airstrip is close to Mastic Point settlement. A small
basin at Mastic Point is provided with a 'wharf' which was built

to meet the needs of vessels serving San Andros plantation. A hotel car meets guests at the San Andros Hotel at Stafford Creek where the water widens for distances greater than two miles between banks and where pine forests, palmettos and scrubs remind some visitors of the Sounds of North Carolina. Yachtsmen select Staniard Creek as a place to anchor not only because of the protection it affords but also for the prevailing east winds which deter insects. The settlement at Staniard Creek extends for nearly two miles. Picturesque small houses and gardens are spread along a sandy beach liberally supplied with coconut palms. Divers congregate further south at Small Hope Bay. The Andros Barrier Reef is only ten minutes away. Divers go there deliberately to 'go over the wall' which divides them from the mile deep Tongue of the Ocean. Fresh Creek, which is around 9 miles south of Staniard is considered to be one of the finest harbours on Andros. Tarpon and bonefish frequent the creek and the reefs outside are favourite haunts of big game fish. Andros Town where the 4000-ft airstrip is located is on the southern side of Fresh Creek. The Andros Yacht Club and the Lighthouse Club were developed there expressly for the excellent fishing. On the other side of the Creek is Coakley Town, a Bahamian settlement.

A 3000-ft airstrip at the northern tip of Mangrove Cay alongside the settlement of Moxey Town gives access to the central region of Andros by air. Two miles from Moxey Town the Commissioner has a residence and office near the dock at Mangrove Cay settlement. On the traditional bank holiday of the first Monday in August, sloops from neighbouring cays and other ports of Andros meet to compete in an annual regatta. Further south on Mangrove Cay beside the waters of the South Bight Bahamian boat builders construct some of the sloops which compete in the Out Island Regatta.

Congo Town, the newest of all airports on Andros, is approximately half an hour's flying time from Nassau. Its construction has made it possible for American visitors to leave Miami 180 miles to the northwest and fly direct to South Andros, where the Las Palmas hotel makes splendid promises. The ocean can be heard 'singing in a shell', the sun can be seen 'walking across the waves', and there is music to be heard from the throat of 'an orange and purple bird perched on a coconut palm'. Towards dawn, which is always the best time to be up and doing on a tropical island, there will be a 'covey of quail flying' and as you walk along 'beaches bleached white by centuries of sunshine' you can meditate, unhindered by man-made noises upon the un-polluted beauty which has survived on Andros because of its centuries of neglect since the age of discovery. The Las Palmas hotel is situated two miles south of Drigg's Hill, which is the northernmost settlement on South Andros. Kemps' Bay, which lies halfway going south along the east coast of South Andros, may be considered as the furthest outpost of civilisation on this end of the island. There live the Commissioner for South Andros and the doctor in charge of the local clinic. Excellent fishing may be enjoyed around the cays in the extreme south of the island where some of the finest types of coral formations are seen.

SUMMARY :– *The Biminis, The Berries, Andros*

THE BIMINIS :	Land area 9 square miles
	Population over 1500
Location :	54 nautical miles from Miami
Airport :	5000 ft on South Bimini. Port of entry for the Bahamas.
Seaport :	North Bimini is port of entry for the Bahamas.
Special Note :	Fresh water *is not plentiful* in the Biminis
THE BERRIES :	30 large cays and many small ones, extending from the Northwest Providence Channel 40 miles southwards to a point 28 miles north-west of Nassau Harbour.
Land and sea area :	About 380 square miles.
Special Note :	Popular as fishing grounds, stop-over points between Florida and Nassau, and as private and settlement islands.
CHUB CAY (Southern Berries) :	Has 5000 ft airstrip and marina. Port of entry.

Crown Colony Club :	Offers charter fishing, bonefish boats and guides; has tennis court, skeet and trap range.
LITTLE HARBOUR CAY (Central Berries) :	Completely protected harbour. Pilots, fishing guides, shipwright, supplies of food sometimes available.
GREAT HARBOUR CAY (Northern Berries) :	Largest of the islands
Bullocks Harbour :	Equipped with telecommunications, stores, markets; crawfishing station of the Berries.
Tamboo Marina :	24 hour service, accommodation for 85 yachts up to 130 feet. Charter planes available.
Airstrip :	4200 ft. Port of entry
Golf Course :	18 hole, designed by Joseph Lee.
Where to Stay :	Great Harbour Club
Activities :	Deep sea charters, small boat rentals; tennis, sailing, skin-diving, exploring caves, swimming.
CISTERN CAY (Northern Berries) :	
Airstrip :	2400 feet
ANDROS	Largest of the islands of the Bahamas
Land Area :	2300 square miles
Population :	Under 10,000
Airports of Entry :	San Andros (6000 ft) Andros Town (4000 ft) South Andros (5000 ft)
Other airports :	Andros Central (5000 ft) Mangrove Cay (3000 ft)
Special Notes :	Settlements on 100-mile-long east coast. 120 mile underwater reef on east coast runs parallel to 1000 fathoms Tongue of the Ocean
How to get there :	By air from Florida or Nassau. By private yacht.

Roads: A good road runs between Fresh Creek and the north. Road building is continuing on Mangrove Cay and South Andros.

Activities: Hunting, fishing, scuba-diving, swim tours, loafing, sailing, birdwatching.

5 New Providence and Grand Bahama

The attractions of New Providence are obvious to the very rich who have acquired palatial homes in the millionaires' enclave at Lyford Cay, on Paradise island, or along the western and eastern shores of the northern coast of New Providence. Nassau is well connected to the outside world by air and sea and for more than a century its mild climate in the winter months has lured escapists from the icy temperatures of northern lands. Surrounded by trusted, well-paid servants, and with larders, 'deep-freezes', and cellars liberally stacked with the world's finest imported food and drink visiting millionaires and their families and friends can rely each year on extended summers of three to four months' duration in their luxury homes on New Providence. They can rely too on daily rounds of golf, while yachts or cruisers from private or public marinas are available for fishing, diving or loafing at sea. In the evenings informal open-air dining is available in private patios perfumed by sweet-scented, night blooming flowers or in the splendid setting of Café Martinique or other favoured restaurants. What the millionaires can do expensively at any time of the year is beyond the reach of most visitors to New Providence. Those who go anywhere in the Bahamas at any time of the year ought to enjoy comfortable incomes if they want to do more than soak up sun on the beaches. Between mid-November and mid-April prices are designed to obtain maximum profits from those who are able to contribute indirectly to the lower cost holidays which are offered during the other months of the year. The island of New Providence is particularly suited because of its highly developed tourist infra-structure to appeal through its Goombay summer programme to travellers who want to enjoy the amenities which are priced beyond their reach in the winter months. Inclusive tour costs include transportation to and from New Providence, transportation to and from airport and sometimes special excursions by sea and land. Further savings are made by the reductions which hoteliers give to guests who buy the 'packaged' holidays which are offered by specialist tour operators. Those who decide on a New Providence holiday ought however to realise that ordinary prices throughout the year reflect the heavy dependence of the island upon imports from the United States. Spending outside the ranges provided by the package tour can be very costly, even for simple items like a glass of beer. Costs are inflated too by the Bahamian tradition of tipping, which is expected never to fall below 15 per cent. The cheapest way of getting around is on foot, but bicycles may be rented at a daily rate which is roughly equivalent to the price of a taxi from a west coast hotel to central Nassau.

The most spectacular sight of Nassau is the modern Potter's Cay Bridge which connects the waterfront to the $3\frac{1}{2}$-mile-long Paradise island. For centuries this island was called Hog and its chief function was that of a natural breakwater protecting the only safe entrance to Providence island. The Bridge, which was built by Resorts International as part of a $56 million development inclusive of marina, hotels, restaurant and casino, has a high water clearance of 70 feet. The first owner to embellish Hog island with a modern home was Dr Axel Wenner-Gren of Sweden. He later sold it to an American multi-millionaire Mr Huntington Hartford, who called it Paradise. The Augustinian cloister which Huntington Hartford brought over from France was originally built by monks at Montrejau long before Columbus set out on his journey to the Indies. In front of the Cloister, gardens run down in seven terraces to the sea. Each terrace is decorated with statues, one dating back to the twelfth century, others recording more modern personages like Franklin D. Roosevelt, Dr Livingstone and the Empress Josephine of France. The Holiday Inn on Paradise Island has replaced the Water Tower on Fort Fincastle as the highest point in the immediate vicinity of Nassau. Casuarinas and coconut trees surround the modern complex of the 45-slip Hurricane Hole Marina which offers amenities and relaxation within full view of the splendid arched Potters Cay Bridge. On the other side of the bridge is Paradise Island Shipyard and Marina. Close by is a ramp for seaplanes. Simplicity and sophistication blend harmoniously on Paradise Island where the landscape comprises beach, coppices, tree bordered avenues and miniature parks as well as 'imported' old style and modern structures. Hog Island has a large casino where gambling is allowed day and night. Professional entertainers perform for guests who can eat in restaurants which remain open until the early hours of the morning. A favourite dining place is the Café Martinique which borders Paradise Lake. Some of the scenes of the film of Ian Fleming's *Thunderball* were set in the grounds of Café Martinique. A charge of $2 is levied upon users of Potters Cay Bridge. Undoubtedly the fee discourages many residents of New Providence from going over to Paradise, but the island's atmosphere of 'out-island' charm is thereby preserved. Otherwise the splendid Cabbage Beach and the more popular Paradise Beach would soon become as 'shopworn' as some of the beaches which lie close to Nassau's harbour.

The title of Nassau was first used to replace 'Charles Town' as the principal settlement on Providence soon after William of Orange succeeded his uncle James II on the English throne in 1688. The original Nassau was a principality which was privately owned by William. In Oldmixon's account of the British Empire in 1708 Hog Island is described as the property of Governor Trott whose period of office on Providence terminated in 1697. By Governor Trott's time a church had already been built in the town of Nassau and he began to erect a fort in the middle of the square where his house stood. This fort was mounted with 28 guns and some demi-culvers. When Peter Henry Bruce, a military engineer who had served Peter the Great of Russia, was sent out in 1741 by the British Authorities to fortify Nassau against threat of Spanish invasion he discovered that Trott's fort which had been built of wood was ready to tumble down and that there were no more than 16 guns resting on very bad carriages.

Fort Charlotte was built a little before the outbreak of the French Revolution in 1789. It was intended to guard the western approach to the harbour of Nassau and was provided with a moat and dungeons. Its chief use today is as a setting for nightly Son-et-Lumière productions. Tours around the fort are conducted by guides who wear 'Zouave uniforms' exactly like those which Queen Victoria personally selected as ceremonial dress for her British West India Regiments.

Near to Fort Charlotte at Ardastra Gardens about 50 flamingos are 'drilled' before feeding time twice daily (at 11 am and 4 pm) by Mr Hedley Edwards, who expects women visitors to be suitably dressed for this performance. Many tourists who visit Ardastra Gardens take their cameras with them for they are unlikely to see flamingos elsewhere in the Bahamas unless they go far south to Inagua. Adjoining Ardastra Gardens is the Seafloor Aquarium where sea lions and dolphins perform several times daily and at 4 pm on Sundays. At the Aquarium scenes from the Bahamian reefs are arranged for the benefit of visitors who are shown sharks, giant turtles, rays, porpoises and eels swimming round in large tanks. Bahamian souvenirs, including tortoiseshell articles made on the spot, are also offered for sale.

The character of Nassau was greatly changed by an enlargement of the harbour of Nassau which was completed in 1969 at a cost of over 20 million Bahamian dollars. The project included deepening of the Channel, removal of part of the natural bar at the entrance, two new breakwaters and a new dock. At the same time the artificial island of Arawak Cay was formed. In August 1973 the government announced that at least three hotels and a convention centre were to be started on the man-made Arawak Cay by a development consortium in which the government was a shareholder. Plans called for the whole island to be developed as a self-contained resort and entertainment complex.

All but the largest ocean-going liners can come alongside the Prince George Wharf. From the wharf a road leads directly to Rawson Square which was named for the man who governed the Bahamas between 1864 and 1869. A visitor to Nassau in 1888 recorded that 'Rawson Square is crowded all day long and even the dogs and cats go down to see the passengers arrive'. Today Rawson Square still attracts visitors. It is also a favourite parking place for horse-drawn 'surrey' vehicles in which sightseers who do not want to explore Nassau on foot, are taken to see the main points of interest.

A favourite stop on the 'surrey' route is the Queen's staircase, a flight of 65 steps which rise steeply from the top of Elizabeth Avenue to the ruins of Fort Fincastle above. The 'staircase' was hewn out of the coral rock in order to provide swift passage for troops from the fort to the sea. Charlotte, wife of George III, is the Queen commemorated in the title. Her name is explicitly mentioned in the title of Fort Charlotte which was erected at the western end of the hill. Fort Fincastle was named after the Governor, the Earl of Dunmore who was responsible for the erection of Fort Fincastle and Fort Charlotte. Before he succeeded to the Earldom his title was Viscount Fincastle. The commanding position of Fort Fincastle made it useful as a signal station. A lift takes visitors to the top of the Water Tower which stands 216 feet above sea level behind the ruins of the Fort.

The name of another governor of the Bahamas, Fitzwilliam is recalled in 'Mt Fitzwilliam', the hill above Nassau on which Governor John Halkett laid the foundations of today's Government House in 1801. Many changes and embellishments have been made since then. The gardens at Government House were designed during the period 1898 to 1904 when Sir Gilbert Carter was Governor. Lady Carter was a native of Boston and her love of beauty is still remembered in Barbados, where she lived at Ilaro Court and contributed greatly to the improvement of Queen's Park gardens. The statue of Christopher Columbus which stands in front of the Governor General's House was made in London, under the supervision of Washington Irving for General Sir James Carmichael Smith, who presented it to the people of the Bahamas. Queen Victoria is honoured by a marble statue which stands between the House of Assembly and the Law Courts. The mace was made in 1799 by Lewis Pantin of St Martins-le-Grand London. It was *not* brought over from South Carolina, but was ordered by the House of Assembly in 1798, when the Speaker was also desired to 'provide a black silk gown with proper trimmings'. Behind the lawcourts shaded by trees is the octagon shaped library which in earlier days was used as a prison. The Royal Victoria Gardens, overlook the the Library. They were designed as an integral part of the Royal Victoria Hotel which was built for $130,000 in the palmy blockade-running days of the American Civil War. The hotel survived periods of affluence and hard times until the late nineteen-sixties when it closed. Over 300 varieties of tropical plants have been introduced into the gardens, which are made conspicuous by an ancient silk cotton tree. The police Band gives public concerts near this tree at advertised times.

Several well-tended homes preserve earlier Colonial styles of town life in central Nassau and on both sides of East Bay Street mellowed mansions recall the high life of certain families who prospered greatly whenever money circulated freely on New Providence. In more modern times residential districts have developed westwards of the city, where architect-designed homes have been built amid small parklands and landscape gardens which provide exclusive privacy for their owners or occupiers. Fox Hill and Adelaide have especial interest as villages which were specifically founded for Africans who were taken by British sailors from foreign slave ships and set free on New Providence. Near Fox Hill village the priest Father Jerome, architect of several Anglican and Catholic churches throughout the Bahamas, designed the school and cloister of St Augustine's monastery. Grant's Town, the nearest 'over the hill' settlement is very close to the heart of the city and is approached through the Gregory Arch close to Government House. Woodes Rogers Walk, named after the Governor who hung nine pirates soon after his arrival in Nassau, is a picturesque waterfront where mailboats and other seagoing craft tie up. An open market runs along the walk where fruit, vegetables and other foodstuffs are daily exposed for sale. The traveller in search of local colour will discover nowhere else in Nassau so many open aspects of the everyday life of the Bahamian.

Bay Street is the main shopping centre of the Bahamas and the commercial heart of Nassau to which people from all parts of New Providence and other islands come for purposes of trade and finance. The roads on either side of Nassau are very good. Views of the sea and offshore islands are frequent. Those who prefer to travel by sea explore 40 acres of Sea Gardens in a glass-bottom boat or take a combined sightseeing and bathing trip across to Paradise Beach. Many hotels make arrangements for sea trips from their piers. A wide variety of sea sports may be enjoyed off New Providence, including 'para-sailing', an elaborate variation of water ski-ing which is preceded by a parachute ride. All the hotels on the beach west of Nassau offer magnificent views of tropical sunsets. Some of these begin as meshes of bluish pink which run into blood-red splashes that soon become mauve swathes draped across greying elephant shaped clouds galloping across the horizon. Not all of the sea front on the northern shores of New Providence has been reserved for tourists. In between the settled areas it laps close beside the road and nowhere more appealingly than obliquely opposite the Traveller's Rest near the village of Gambier. This bar and restaurant is deservedly popular with those who leave the conventional hotel areas to explore other parts of New Providence. In recent years some residents of New Providence have been adding new art forms to the popular crafts of straw, wood and shell work. In the Arts Courtyard, not far from Bay Street, paintings, pottery and fabric designs are made and exposed for sale, and at least once a year in the summer the works of resident painters are displayed in the open streets for any visitor or resident to see, admire or buy.

Horse racing is exclusively a winter sport on New Providence. From early January to mid-April twice-weekly meetings are held on the race track near West Bay Street, which for many years was known as Hobby Horse Race Track.

Evening entertainment is abundant in several hotels near Nassau and on Paradise Island. The range varies between individual vocalist or musician to elaborate reviews at the large Le Cabaret theatre on Paradise island. Native shows at Dirty Dick's, Drumbeat and Junkanoo are popular with visitors who want to get away from hotel settings. Some Bahamian performers like Peanuts Taylor at the Drumbeat or the singers Eloise and Pat Rolle have helped to spread the cult of Goombay (Bahamian version of Calypso) and to establish local songs and entertainment for visitors. Not all Bahamian night clubs lie over the hill. In recent years greater numbers of Bahamian residents are seen at beach hotels like Nassau Beach where barbecues and dances are no longer exclusively arranged for visitors from overseas.

Grand Bahama. When James H. Stark of Boston visited Grand Bahama in 1890 he discovered settlements at McLean's, Carrion Crow Harbour, Freetown, Golden Grove and Eight Mile Rock. The men who lived on Grand Bahama in that year were employed as spongers, fishermen or farmers. Stark was told that settlers first put down roots on Grand Bahama about 1806, but that the island had often been visited before by lumbermen. In his guide book published in 1891 Stark noted abundance of fresh water, an interior suitable for grazing, and 'white lands' along the coasts where 'fair crops of corn' were harvested.

Some 40 years later another visiting writer, Major Bell, discovered a 'lost legion' of men in the vicinity of West End where a simple commissioner and one policeman represented the imperial authority of Britain. Bell in his book, published in 1934, said that this community of adventurers moved hundreds of thousands of dollars of liquor stocks across to the American mainland in a fleet of motor-powered cruisers and about six aeroplanes. He told too of an early promoter who was then advertising Grand Bahama as a haven for Americans who wanted to find cheap and plentiful liquor only twenty minutes flying time from Palm Beach. This man, according to Bell, actually printed leaflets designed to encourage 'cheap booze' flights and he was always talking about 'building a casino'. He was many years ahead of his time for no casino was built until the 'sixties.

An attempt by the Butlin organisation of Britain in the early 'fifties to popularise West End for 'community tourists' was unsuccessful. By 1943 the major impetus to the Grand Bahama's economy was coming from General Seafoods (Bahamas) Ltd, a company engaged in canning and freezing fish.

The giant leap into a twentieth-century world was made in the mid-fifties when the Virginian, Wallace Groves, who had come to Grand Bahama as an executive of the Abaco Lumber Company, obtained for the privately organised Grand Bahama Port Authority the right to develop Freeport area. Groves was supported in this enterprise by Englishman Charles Hayward and another American, Charles Allen. Under the terms of the Hawksbill agreement made between the government of the Bahamas and the Grand Bahama Port Authority investors in real estate and personal property on the island were exempted from taxes on income or capital gains for 35 years. At the same time no customs, excise or stamp duties relative to their investments were to be levied for 99 years. By 1959 the Port Authority had begun operation of a deep-water harbour, which has been enlarged several times since. The landing strip built in the early days of Freeport's construction has been expanded to become an international jetport capable of handling over one million passengers a year.

The developed area of Freeport and Lucaya, which runs between Hawksbill Creek and the United States Missile Tracking Base near Freetown, covers about 234 square miles of an island which is 65 miles long and on average 7 miles wide. Unlike West End, these locations did not evolve but sprang Minerva-like out of the brain of Wallace Groves to meet the requirements of international financiers who could appreciate that Grand Bahama was conveniently located 87 miles from West Palm Beach, 212 miles from Miami and only about 1000 miles from the great money city of New York.

Modern development on Grand Bahama preceded the rise to power of the political party which led the Bahamas into independence on 10 July 1973. Despite some uncertainties arising from changes in political direction, confidence in the economic potential of Grand Bahama has been maintained and reinforced by the Bahamas government's participation as shareholder in the Grand Bahama Port Authority Limited which is now 92.5 per cent owned by Benguet Consolidated Inc. This Philippine-based company, after acquiring control of Wallace Groves' original company, effected a reorganisation of activities in October 1971.

The beginning of modern tourism on Grand Bahama dates from 1964 when the Lucayan Beach Hotel opened. Visitors to Freeport and Lucaya rose from 26,000 in 1963 to half a million in 1972. By then there were 115 miles of paved roads and 600 miles of unpaved roads. Other tourist assets included marinas, restaurants, night clubs, five 18-hole golf courses, an Underwater Explorers Club, a riding stable, tennis courts, sports fields, the ten acre International Bazaar, the Rand Memorial Nature Centre, a botanic garden, schools, churches, shops and public beaches.

Grand Bahama has enough water to supply the needs of a resident population of one quarter of a million and by 1971 the Freeport Power Company had installed generators with a total capacity of 12,000 kilowatts.

Tourism and land development followed upon the industrial development of Freeport which has been centred from the beginning upon the bunkering of ships operating in the Gulf Stream. The Bahamas Oil Refining Company, which is jointly owned by New England Petroleum Corporation and Standard Oil Company of California did not begin operations until 1970, but their site

16 *St Andrew's Presbyterian Church, Nassau*
17 *St Augustine's Monastery, overlooking Nassau*

18 *Sunset over yachts, Marsh Harbour, Great Abaco*
19 *Flamingos in flight over Great Salt Lake, Inagua*

near the harbour is capable of processing half a million tons of crude oil daily for export to the eastern seaboard cities of the United States. At the time of writing plans were far advanced for the establishment of a petro-chemical industry to use the by-products of the refinery. The Bahama Cement Company, a wholly owned subsidiary of US Steel, has invested over $75 million in Freeport and produced around 5 million tons of cement annually, mostly for export. Another multi-million dollar investor in Freeport, the Syntex Corporation processes chemical ingredients for pharmaceutical products and since 1968 has been supplying world markets with the steroid compounds used in oral contraceptives. Other distributive, manufacturing and service companies have established facilities in Freeport which is also well provided with banks and financial institutions.

Profit without taxation has been the incentive which attracted many million dollars of investment to Grand Bahama within 15 years and converted a sleeping Out island into the hearthland of Bahamian industrial enterprise. That initiative was taken by an American, in keeping with a pattern which links Bahamian economic progress more tightly with the American mainland than with any other portion of the globe. Both the Bahamian people and the American people are products of an environment which require a blending of the qualities of pioneers with the spirit of new community dwellers involved in a march of progress. It says much for the 'modern-day pioneers' of Freeport/Lucaya that although they originally came from all over the Bahamas, the Caribbean, North and Central America and Europe they were able to pool their talents in order to forge new communities where none existed before.

The economic expansion of Grand Bahama has not been confined to the boundaries of Freeport and Lucaya. During 1974 Burmah Oil Company Limited, a wholly owned subsidiary of Burmah Oil Company Limited (London), expected to begin operation of a deep-water petroleum terminal which has been carved out of 3000 acres of hitherto unused Crown Land, east of the Bonded Area limits of Freeport. The new terminal and storage facilities have been designed to accommodate tankers up to 350,000 tons and to provide a throughput capacity of 150 million barrels of oil yearly. They were constructed for the Bahamas

G

Government and Seabulk International Corporation of Fort Lauderdale, Florida, who are jointly associated in the enterprise.

The International Underwater Explorers Society of Freeport provides many facilities for divers. At their club a large refill station, a fleet of dive boats and over one hundred tanks are available for rent. Access is sometimes available to Hydrolab, a 16ft by 8ft cylindrical chamber anchored in 45 feet of water.

Halfway between Freeport Harbour and West End an ocean blue hole is located on Deadman's Reef. West End, which lies 25 miles northwest of Hawksbill Creek, was until 1963 the administrative capital of Grand Bahama and is still the seat of one of the resident commissioners on the island. An airport was built at West End in the 'fifties by the Jack Tar Hotel group which took over the Butlin holiday centre and built it into the Grand Bahama Hotel and Country Club.

West End is only 55 miles from Lake Worth Inlet and 67 miles from Fort Lauderdale and is a convenient port of entry for yachtsmen. Skeleton warehouses and half sunk piers along the waterfront recall the days of bootlegging, while coconuts, casuarinas and flowering shrubs straggle raggedly along a village of fishermen's cottages. A main road runs from West End in the northwest right across Grand Bahama as far as McLean's Town in the East. The rest of Grand Bahama territory to the south alternates between cays and creeks. Not far from McLean's Town facing Big Harbour Creek is Deep Water Cay, where a fishing club and cottages are operated by Gilbert Drake of Palm Beach. The Club is served by a 2200 foot grass airstrip, which must only be used after prior notification to the Club.

If there is one thing lacking around Freeport's area it is the absence of regular modern public transportation. Taxi drivers on Grand Bahama model themselves on the taxi drivers of New Providence. Many of them are immigrants from Nassau. They regard all other forms of visitors' transport as threats to their high living standards. Unfortunately some side effects of a taxi monopoly can cause inconvenience to visitors. At the luxury hotel where I stayed several miles from the airport, for example, there was no taxi service and no hotel bus service to get me to the airport in time for an early morning flight to Nassau one

Sunday. Had a friendly Cuban, Captain Sam, not been passing the hotel entrance by chance, I would have had to walk the whole way, and would have lost my reservation.

A further problem for drivers on Sunday is caused by the complete shutdown of petrol stations. These practices are strange on an island catering to over half a million tourists each year, and will undoubtedly change as more mature ideas about service to guests are accepted by the whole community of islanders.

SUMMARY :

New Providence
Area : 21 miles long by 7 miles wide.
Population : Over 105,000.
Yacht Havens : East Bay Yacht Basin (25 berth), Nassau Yacht Haven (100 berths), Bayshore Marina (150 berths), Nassau Harbour Club (65 berths), Hurricane Hole Marina (45 slips), Lyford Cay Harbour (private), Coral Harbour (on southshore, departure point for Andros).
Churches :
Anglican : Christchurch Cathedral, George and King Streets, St Matthews, Shirley Street and Church Lane (oldest); St Mary's, Virginia Street.
Roman Catholic : Our Lady of the Holy Souls, East and Young Street; Sacred Heart, Shirley Street; St Francis Xavier, West Hill (first Catholic church in the Bahamas).
Methodist : Trinity, Frederick Street; Ebenezer, Shirley Street; Wesley, Grant's Town.
Other Religious denominations represented : Baptist, First Church of Christ Scientist, Evangelists, Greek Orthodox, Presbyterian, Salvation Army, Seventh Day Adventists.
Transportation : Taxis; Buses for package tourists, some hotel guests; Surreys; Rental cars; Motorbikes, cycles, scooters, bicycles.
Beaches : Western Esplanada, Saunders Beach, The Caves Beach, Fort Montagu Beach, Paradise Beach, Cable Beach.
Active Sports : Fishing, Golf, Tennis, Skin diving, Boating, Yachting, Water Skiing, Para-Sailing, Private Plane Flying.
Spectator Sports : Soccer, Baseball, Volleyball, Squash, Softball.

Recreation: Guided Underwater Reef Tours, Seafloor Aquarium, Flamingo Parade, Glass Bottom boat trips.
Special Event: Alternate Saturdays, Changing the Guard at Government House 10 am.
Entertainment: Hotel Nightspots, Native Clubs, elaborate reviews, gambling.
Meals: Three types, luxury, unpretentious, native.
Examples:
Luxury: Café Martinque.
Unpretentious: Howard Johnson's (Nassau Beach).
Bahamian: Traveller's Rest.
Shopping:
Imported goods: cameras, china, coins, crystal, linens, liquor, perfume, silver, watches, woollens.
Local: Hats, baskets, bags and other straw goods, tortoiseshell, wood carvings, shellwork.
Shopping Hours: 9 am to 5 pm Monday to Saturday (some shops close on Friday or Saturday in afternoon).
Banking Hours: Mondays to Thursdays 9 am to 7 pm. Fridays 9 am to 1 pm and 4 pm to 6 pm.
Service Clubs: Rotary Club of Nassau (Tuesday Sheraton British); Nassau East (Friday Flagler Inn); Nassau West (Sonesta Beach Hotel); Inner Wheel Club; Kiwanis; Lions.
Medical Facilities: Modern.
Laundry: Most hotels provide.
Departure Tax: 12 years and over $3; 3 to 12 years $1.50.
Dress: Evening wear coat and tie. No swimwear in central Nassau.
Driving: On left, foreign driving licences valid for 3 months only.
Places to see outside Nassau: Country villages to Gambier, Adelaide, Fox Hill and Carmichael. Bacardi Rum Factory, near Coral Harbour. Clifton Pier dock and desalinating plant. Lyford Cay peninsula. Jumbey Villages, Blue Hill Road, thatched huts, barns, kitchens. Angelo's Art Centre, Harold Road: sculpture, pottery, figurines (open Monday to Saturday 9 am to 5 pm).
Golf Courses: (18 holes) Coral Harbour, Paradise Island Golf Club, Sonesta Beach Hotel Golf Course; South Ocean Golf Club, Lyford Cay Golf Club (private) (9 hole) Blue Hill Golf Club.

Bahamia Museum, East Street: Monday to Saturday 9 am to 5 pm, Sunday 9 am to 1 pm.

Grand Bahama

Area: 430 square miles.
Population: Over 26,000.
Information Centre: Ministry of Tourism International Bazaar, open Monday to Saturday 9.30 am to 5 pm.
Transport Rentals: Hertz, Avis, National, Budget for cars, Island Scooter Rentals for motor scooters.
Bus Tours: 3 hours daily, except Sundays and holidays.
Glass Bottom Boat Tours: Leave Oceanus Hotel daily at 10 am, noon and 2 pm.
Horseback Beach Rides: Pinetree Stables daily at 9 am, 11 am 2 pm, 3.30 pm.
Shopping: International Bazaar 10 am to 6 pm Mondays to Saturdays.
Rand Memorial Nature Centre: 100 acres of woodland, twice daily guided tours.
Garden of the Groves: 11 acres near Shannon Country Club.
English Pubs: Sir Winston Churchill (Ranfurly Circus); Pub on the Mall (Mall at Sunrise); Britannia Pub (King's Road on Bell Channel).
Independent Night Clubs: Jokers Wild (Midshipman Road); Goombay Club (off Queen's Highway); House of Lords (midshipman Road); Ruby Club (off West Sunrise Highway).
Restaurants: The Bahamas Ministry of Tourism lists over 50 places in its leaflet on where to dine in Freeport. Excellent international cuisine is obtainable in restaurants of the International Bazaar, in hotels, and in special locations like the Sir Winston Churchill or the Stoned Crab at Taino Beach.
Golf Courses:
Freeport: Bahama Reef Golf and Country Club; King's Inn and Golf Club; Lucayan Golf and Country Club; Shannon Golf and Country Club.
West End: Grand Bahama Hotel and Country Club.
Churches: Mary Star of the Sea (Catholic), Tamarind Street; Ang-

lican Episcopal Church, East Atlantic Drive; St Paul's Methodist Church, Beachway Drive; Lutheran Church, East Sunrise Highway; First Baptist Church, Nansen Avenue; Freeport Hebrew synagogue.

Airports: Freeport; West End.

Airstrip: Grass, on Deep Water Cay.

6 The Abacos

The Abacos comprise a multiplicity of cays scattered around their northeastern approaches and surrounding large segments of the western and eastern shores of the two main islands of Little Abaco and Great Abaco. The collective land area of the Abacos is 650 square miles and its small world of islands extends over 130 miles of sea. The southernmost point of the archipelago lies 75 miles to the north of Nassau. Miami is located 200 miles to the West.

The most northerly of the developed Abaco Cays is Walker's Cay. A fishing club began operations there as long ago as 1939. It is now used by the Walker's Cay Club. The Cay has two airstrips. Mr Robert H. Ablanalp, the proprietor of Walker's Cay, has established a marine breeding station on the island.

There is a settlement of about 150 people near the harbour of Grand Cays, which is a port of entry for the Bahamas. Bonefish abound in the shallow flats of their sands and lagoons. Good guides live in the harbour area.

Further south is another archipelago collectively described as the Double Breasted Cays. Less well known than the Exuma cays this strangely named archipelago is just as beautiful and is surrounded by waters of many hues which flow past the varied landpatterns.

A United States missile station has been established on Little Carter Cay. A 400-ft mast is visible from the sea up to five miles away. Fishermen from Little Abaco also use Little Carter Cay at certain periods of the year.

One of the best harbours north of Green Turtle Cay is formed by the natural junction of Allan's and Pensacola Cays. The southeastern tip of Pensacola Cay has an almost completely land-locked harbour. A tall radio mast is visible up to 20 miles from the sea. The Cay is privately owned.

A narrow causeway connects Little Abaco to Great Abaco in the neighbourhood of Angel Fish Point. Spanish Cay is another privately owned island with an airstrip eastwards of Angel Fish Point. Powell Cay, south of Spanish Cay, is also privately owned. It has long stretches of beach and rises to a height of 100 feet above sea level. Obliquely opposite, on the neck of Great Abaco island, is Cooper's Town, which has a school and some attractive houses set among coconut palms by the seashore. Paradise Hill Hotel overlooks the bay and provides Bahamian style rooms and cuisine. A few miles to the southeast of Powell Cay, development has taken place on one of the privately owned Ambergris Cays.

Green Turtle Cay is one of the best known islands of the Abacos because of New Plymouth, a village which Americans consider to be a small replica of New Plymouth, Massachusetts as they imagine it to have been 150 years ago. The island is $3\frac{1}{2}$ miles long and in some places $1\frac{1}{2}$ miles wide. It is an island of brightly painted houses, paved lanes and tropical flowers. It is connected to Great Abaco by water taxis which offer regular service across a two mile strip of water from Green Turtle Cay. Treasure Cay has a resident Commissioner and clinic with a resident nurse. A doctor visits weekly from Marsh Harbour. On July 4th Green Turtle Cay is the setting for an annual regatta and at all times of the year yachtsmen are welcome at shore establishments which have been especially designed for their comfort. The main dock is on Black Sound. In the centre of New Plymouth an inn of that name has survived for more than 130 years. Sea food is excellent there as it is in many other inns and restaurants of the Abacos. South of Green Turtle Cay, a coconut studded island with a good beach is described by Abaconians as a typical 'South Sea island'. No Name Cay to its south is privately owned.

Treasure Cay is a peninsula attached to the main island of Abaco. The development of Treasure Cay began in 1961 when about 1400 acres of crown land was obtained on lease, By May 1965 the company which obtained the lease had completed a small hotel by the beach, partially dredged out a marina, laid out some roads, erected a few cottages and made provision for electricity and water supplies. A small overgrown narrow track then led to 'Green Turtle Airport'. There were no shops, doctor, school nor shipping services, progress was slow until 1968 when a small community at Treasure Cay acquired a doctor, a clinic and also a mini-market. In May of that year Deltec International Limited, in association with three British merchant banks, acquired Treasure Cay Limited. The pace of growth was immediate. By 1972 there were 167 privately owned houses landscaped amid groves of casuarinas and other Bahamian trees. Today Treasure Cay has a sizeable resident community for whom an elementary school, medical facilities, a shopping centre, a power station and other services have been provided. In addition Treasure Cay Beach Hotel and Garden Villas offer 155 rooms, swimming pools, tennis courts and an 18-hole championship golf course with a superbly situated hilltop clubhouse and restaurant. The hotel at Treasure Cay combines luxury with informality. The food is excellent and the service friendly. The hotel's Night Club, the Crow's Nest, shares in a general elegance of atmosphere, while the ground floor shop contains a selection of books on the Bahamas second only to those of the best bookshops of Nassau. Treasure Cay's abundant supply of good fresh water is piped throughout the development area. This water is also available and free to vessels making use of the 40-berth marina.

By early 1973 a new Catholic church had been constructed by a wealthy American in memory of his parents and plans were far advanced for expansion of the sewage system and introduction of a dental clinic. New development projects had also been started. Overall investment in the development area was then assessed at 20 million dollars.

The relaxed and serene environment at Treasure Cay is nowhere more evident than at the airport, which seems as far 'away from it all' as a remote railway station in the heart of North Wales. The airport manager was a 'hymn-singing' lady from Green Turtle Cay, a genuine white Bahamian 'conch' and her husband, a cheerful grinning 65-year-old white porter, had plenty of time, after shifting a handful of suitcases for a dozen feet, to talk of his adventures on the mainland of America and at home. Like his hymn-singing wife he accepted with regret England's decision to leave Abaco under the flag of the newly independent Commonwealth of the Bahamas. 'They don't seem to want us', he said. 'Nothing we can do about it'. While his wife sang hymns he told me how many times he was bitten by turtles and how the hotel on Treasure Cay couldn't buy all the pawpaws he could grow on Green Turtle Cay.

Loneliness is a big factor in the Bahamian way of life. The friendliness of Out islanders throughout the Bahamas derives from the fact that there is always time for people to talk to one another. To be silent is to be unfriendly.

Great Guana Cay, which resembles an elongated daschshund, which has lost its tail to Scotland Cay, lies between Whale and Man of War Cays. White sandy beaches run along both sides of the narrow island. On November 5 a Guy Fawkes Day Regatta is followed by a wild boar barbecue and burning of the guy. The small settlement amid coconuts and casuarinas, has a church, hotel and school. Water taxis run services from Marsh Harbour and small planes can fly by arrangement to the airstrip on Scotland Cay three miles distant.

Spread about between Great Guana Cay and the mainland of Great Abaco island are a group of rocky islets of which Foots Cay is the most prominent. The 2000-ft airstrip on Scotland Cay was built to accommodate winter residents who have built homes on an island which has good soils and fine beaches conveniently close to the fishing grounds of Fish Cays.

At Man of War Cay a community of boat and ship builders produces excellent dinghies and outboard hulls at competitive prices. Fishing and cultivation of garden produce and fruits are other activities of this integrated group of Bahamians whose houses, stores and general amenities proclaim their achievement and high standards of living. Daily services between Marsh Harbour, Hope Town, and Man of War are provided by scheduled water taxis operated by Marcel and Richie Albury. The Dock'n Dine at the head of Albury's Dock is renowned throughout the Bahamas for its excellent sea food at reasonable prices.

Marsh Harbour is the most highly developed town of the Abacos. The innocence of Marsh Harbour is largely that of people who have made a myth of their past. It stems from the needs of transplanted men and women to push down roots in the land of their adoption. It is the innocence of the descendants of European farmers and fisherfolk whose memories are of lands and people with whom they have had no lasting relationships for centuries.

Their uprooted forefathers first put down new roots in the North American colonies, but they had refused at the time of the great American Rebellion to give up their allegiance to the British throne. They had instead gone to Out-islands of the Bahamas deliberately to preserve and maintain all the rights and privileges of English freemen which had been promised them by the English monarchs when charters were granted to respective proprietors of American plantations. Only, they believed, by remaining loyal to the English throne could they enjoy freedom from political dictation by persons who no longer cherished those rights. Innocent pride in their 'Loyalist' origins is accompanied by a sense of purpose which is engendered by a self-reliance natural to those whose survival depends on primary skills. This sense of purpose is evident to anyone who lands on Marsh Harbour's airport after visiting some of the other family islands. I was delighted to share a Volkswagen with other passengers, relieved to discover that I was not compelled to hire a huge Detroit Chariot as in Freeport or Nassau. It was amusing too, to hear the conversations which passed over the radio link to which all taxis, airports, hotels and many private subscribers are linked. The white taxi driver was a man of substance. At least he lived in a smart modern house which in England would denote an income of over £3000 a year. He was not the only one. Before I left Marsh Harbour I met a smiling black taxi-driver who plied for hire during the week but whose occupation on Sundays was to minister to the spiritual needs of his black congregation. His meeting house was one of the smartest buildings in the new city of Marsh Harbour. He told me that he preached a simple Pentecostal faith which showed the way to heaven.

Despite the apparent success of this smiling minister who did not disdain to work for a living on weekdays it is plain that the quality of life is not the same for blacks and whites at Marsh Harbour. Indeed the waterfront divides unequally between the houses of the most prosperous whites and the dwellings of the blacks. Most of the houses on the white side have well tended gardens, while those of the blacks reflect differences of attitudes and culture patterns. Hovels are more visible on the black side of the waterfront. At the very end of the black strip one relatively large mansion proclaims the economic independence of its owner. Some of the successful white commercial men like 'Daddy Roberts' built modern West Indian style mansions in new residential districts which had marked the town's expansion. Daddy Roberts later left for Australia but the house remains as an indication of the relatively simple life style of an Out island merchant leader. Much more sophisticated homes have been built by outsiders on the long neck of the Eastern shores. Conspicuous on raised ground is the turreted green turquoise castle built by Evans Cottman, the 'Out Island Doctor'.

At Treasure Cay I had been told how to catch a turtle by the fisherman porter from Green Turtle Cay. In Marsh Harbour at the Conch Inn, an intimate family restaurant serving excellent food and drink, an Abaconian instructed me in the art of hunting the boar. The first requirement, he said, is a well trained hunting dog. He knows how and when to corner a boar so that the hunter can tie its legs together and lift it into a van for transport to his home, where a knife can be used to extinguish life. A boar caught wild is solid profit for a hunter because his only expenditure is on transport. A pig bred at home instead has to be fed many meals before it can be converted into pork. Profit on a wild boar might be as much as $120. Boar hunting is however a dying sport on Abaco, where wild boars are gradually disappearing as they did very early on Barbados.

The essential appeal of the Abaconian way of life is likely to continue for many years more. The people who have settled on the main islands and cays of the Abacos love nature and a pace of life which is opposed to the bustle of big cities. Each newcomer selects a pattern of his choice and proceeds to weave a web of life. If he stays long enough the island's gravitational pull will gradually draw him into its own fields of force. The siren songs of the Abacos cannot easily be resisted by those who have put down deep roots. The visitor who stays only a few days or a few weeks instead can savour charms and take away pleasant memories which are produced by a combination of climate, vegetation and people. Some of the memories will surely be of refreshing dawns, sweet bird songs, the slap of the ocean wave on pink sands, the perfume of flowers and the music of trade winds ruffling casuarinas or coconut fronds.

Marsh Harbour has an old club house set in spacious grounds facing the sea. German investors were about to develop the site as a modern resort complex at the time of my visit in 1973. If it is developed a new impetus will be given to Marsh Harbour's prospects as a holiday town. Already Don Dawes' Lofty Fig Inn, a small complex of self-service cottages set around a swimming pool, is as appealing as any similar types of accommodation in the Caribbean and very good value for money. The Conch Inn run by the Smith family of Montreal is a meeting place for the residents of the Lofty Fig where they can sample the best Bahamian dishes while soaking up the atmosphere of a very small world. Caribbean Sailing Yachts Limited, a company which advertises itself as the Caribbean leader in bareboats has its headquarters at Marsh Harbour. Besides the Out-islands practitioner, Marsh Harbour has two doctors who have charge of medical clinics and a resident dentist. The community is served by a broadcast network which is used by more than 200 subscribers.

At Elbow Cay, formerly known as Little Guano Cay across the water from Marsh Harbour, the most conspicuous landmark is a 'Candy-rock' striped lighthouse which lies close to a picture post-card type settlement of gaily painted cottages and stores. A small bareboat fleet is maintained on the west creek. Hope Town Harbour Lodge is set among a clump of tall coconut palms and casuarina trees near the old style 'New England seaport village' from which it takes its name. Also popular on Elbow Cay is the Club of that name. It has a dockside, twelve rooms for rental and a cuisine which reflects the Scandinavian origin of its Danish husband-and-wife team of managers. Tilloo Cay, a narrow strip of land four miles long, separates the Pelican Cays from the privately owned Lynyard Cay to the south. On its sheltered west coast are some fine beaches and places to anchor. On the leeside of the ocean Pelican Cays are frequently pounded by heavy surf. Animal life on and around the cays is protected by regulations which are administered through the National Trust. Their efforts have been strengthened by the support of the owner of Cornish Cay which lies near the mainland off Spencer's Bight.

Claw-shaped Little Harbour, which lies southwest of Lynyard Cay on the outward edge of the Bight of Old Robinson, is worth a visit. It is the home of Mr and Mrs Randolph Johnston, both of whom have established themselves as artists in the Bahamas. Mr Johnston works in bronze and his wife makes ceramic and glazed metal articles. The Johnston's schooner, which has been converted into Pete's Deckhouse Pub, is used as a social centre by Little Harbour's small community. The almost circular harbour is mostly surrounded by white beach and there are high cliffs with caves on the western side. About 20 'boiling holes', which penetrate deeply underground to join the tides of the ocean, have been discovered between the many cays of Little Harbour Creek, where fishing is good. A high coastline runs between Little Harbour and Cherokee settlement six miles to the south west. At Ocean Hill, it rises to 120 feet above sea level. Cherokee has a post office and telephone station for the use of its small community of shipbuilders and fishermen. A lighthouse at Hole in the Wall denotes the southern end of Great Abaco. It is approximately 26 miles south of Little Harbour and 47 miles north east of Nassau. The western shores of Abaco have relatively few settlements and movement by sea in the 'Bight' is much less than off the eastern coasts. Sandy Point is the most westerly settlement in the extreme south. It has extensive groves of coconut palms and casuarinas and many gaily painted houses set around flower gardens. Sandy Point is a port of entry for the Bahamas and has a post office with direct communications to Nassau and the United States. A fleet of sloops is maintained by the resident fishermen. A fuel dock and general store supplies visiting yachtsmen. The central government keeps a commissioner at Sandy Point and maintains a school with a roll of 150 pupils. About eight miles to the northwest is Gorda Cay, which has a private 2400-ft paved airstrip, two natural harbours and good beaches. There is a small settlement on the island. Further north is Mores Island, which rises to 110 feet in the north and has two picturesque village settlements Hard Bargain and The Bight, with a combined population of over 400. The Marls, which are a cluster of innumerable small cays which extend for about 20 miles, connect with the Woolendean Cays and Joe Downer Cays off the northwestern shores of Great Abaco. From the air the cays resemble liquid craters connected by thin strips of white marl. The Marls to the east of Joe Downer Cays are favourite nesting places for cormorants. North of Joe Downer Cays on the mainland below Davis Point a logging camp at Norman's Castle was open until 1929. It is now deserted by human beings, although visited by hogs and wild horses. Deep water surrounds most of the steep cliffs which rise up sheer from the sea at Basin Harbour Cay. They have been shaped by wind and weather through the centuries into weird figures which look like men and animals. Pine woods and palm trees cover several of the island's valleys and hillsides. There are two harbours, Basin and East End.

Randall's Cay, a long island with high cliffs, lies near the tips of Little and Great Abaco. On the mainland of Little Abaco about 4½ miles from Randall's Cay sisal was once cultivated. The land rises up at Black Point to join groves of inland pines which grow right up to the peaks.

The bonefishing flats north of the low flat Mangrove Cay are popular with fishermen.

SUMMARY:

The Abacos
Population: About 8000.
Extent: About 130 miles of uncounted islets and cays.
Size: 650 square miles.
Location: 200 miles east of Miami, 75 miles north of Nassau.
Accommodation at: Cherokee Sound, Great Guana Cay, Green Turtle Cay, Elbow Cay, Man-o'-War Cay, Marsh Harbour, Treasure Cay, Cooper's Town, Walker's Cay.
Air Services: Daily to Treasure Cay and Marsh Harbour from Miama. Fort Lauderdale and West Palm Beach, Bahamasair scheduled services from Miami, Freeport and Nassau. Charter and private flights.
Airports: Walker's Cay, Treasure Cay, Marsh Harbour, Gorda Cay, Sandy Point.
Movement within the Abacos: Charter boats, ferry service, private plane, taxis, bicycles, car rentals.
Sports: Fishing, sailing, cruising, hunting, skindiving, diving, tennis (Treasure Cay), golf (18-hole golf course at Treasure Cay).
National Park: Pelican Cays.
Largest Island: Great Abaco (approximately 100 miles long by

20 miles at widest point). Good road between Treasure Cay peninsula and commercial centre at Marsh Harbour.

Fauna : Birds, wild ponies, wild hogs, ducks, pigeons.

Charter Boats Available : at Green Turtle Cay, Treasure Cay, Elbow Cay, Marsh Harbour, Walker's Cay.

Docks and Fuel Facilities : at Elbow Cay, Man-o'-War Cay, Marsh Harbour, Treasure Cay, Walker's Cay, White Sound Harbour, Sandy Point

Ports of Entry : Grand Cay, Treasure Cay, Marsh Harbour, Sandy Point.

Abaco Businessmen Association : Marsh Harbour.

Land and Sea Park : Pelican Cays.

21 (top) *The Waterfront, Tarpum Bay, Eleuthera*
22 (above) *Houses, Tarpum Bay*

7 Eleuthera and its Islands

Spaniards for centuries regarded the Lucayan islands of the 'low seas' as legally theirs by right of discovery. By 1513, according to Don Pietro Martire, a member of the Spanish Council of the Indies, they had 'explored 406 of the islands' and 'carried off 40,000 of both sexes as slaves'.

Some of the islands are shown in early maps. In 1500 Juan de la Cosa indicated Habacoa, Yumey (Exuma). Guanahani (San Salvador), Mamana (Rum Cay), Samana (Long Island), Saomete (Crooked Island) and Yucaya (Caicos). Twelve islands were shown in the Turin map of 1523. The islands were known to English sailors long before the end of the first Elizabethan era. Sir John Hawkins' brother William navigated the seas between Cuba and some islands of the Bahamas in 1583. Two years later a group of English settlers on their way to Raleigh's Roanoake island in North America made a temporary stop at Caicos. No English claim to the islands was made, however, until the second decade of the seventeenth century, when England's Attorney General, Sir Robert Heath, petitioned King Charles I for a grant of American lands, inclusive of the low sea islands.

Sir Robert had received the order of knighthood a few years after his election to the House of Commons in 1620. As Solicitor General he had to defend the royal prerogative against determined attacks by the rising middle class parliamentarians. His authority was greatly increased by appointment in 1625 to the office of Attorney General and on 1 June 1627 he appeared before the King's Council to lay an elaborate answer to the Commons' Petition of Right. Later he conducted major Star Chamber prosecutions against prominent members of the Commons. Heath's championship of the royal prerogative at home was matched by his ambition to see a greater England overseas, an expanding England which could match or perhaps surpass the achievements

H

of the Spanish Empire or at the very least hold its own with an powerful emerging Dutch state. On 30 October 1629 Charles I gave Heath nearly 500 miles of American lands, overlapping parts of Virginia and running southwards to a point within two day's march of the Spanish fort of St Augustine. Tacked on to this grant were 'the islands of Veajus and Bahama and all other islands to the south'. A precedent for this tacking of islands on to a mainland charter had been set by James I when he included the islands which had been discovered by Juan Bermudez in 1515 and which were known as the 'Bermuthes' or 'Bermudas', in an extended charter of the Virginia company.

Heath may have wanted the low-sea islands as potential sources of salt, dyewoods, timber and fish, or he may merely have wished to secure them before they were sought by some other influential courtier or merchant syndicate. In the event he did nothing to develop them.

The French were early rivals of the English in the West Indies. They had disputed Carlisle's claim to the Caribbees by settling on his island of St Christopher, and in 1633 Richelieu challenged Heath's title to the low sea islands by obtaining a Royal grant of the Bahama islands for Guillaume de Caen who was at the same time raised to the nobility as Baron des Bahames.

We do not know what were Heath's reactions to the French claims to his Royal grant in the Bahamas. His own popularity at the English Court seems to have been falling in these years because of the circulation of rumours to the effect that he was secretly in sympathy with Puritan aims. He was removed from office in 1634 and was only restored to Royal favour in 1636 when he was appointed King's Sergeant. His loyalty to the King resulted in promotion to the office of Chief Justice, but he was later impeached by the House of Commons for high treason. All his estates were sequestered in 1645 and he had to flee to France in 1646. He was still a refugee in that country when he died.

It was on the day after Heath's death that the Rump Parliament, which had been responsible for the execution of Charles I on January 30, passed an act on behalf of the Adventurers for the Eleutherian islands. These Adventurers were a group of London merchants and members of Parliament brought together by William Sayle, an experienced agent of the Somers Islands company which had bought the Virginia company's rights to the Bermudas. Sayle had been appointed a member of the Bermuda Council in 1630 and was later promoted to the post of governor by the Somers Islands Company. Bermuda's sailors passed regularly through the Bahamas by 1640 on their way to North American ports and reports of the islands they saw must have excited the curiosity of Sayle, whose small Bermudian empire was ringed around by an irregular oval of no more than 22 miles in length and about 3 miles in width. By contrast Eleuthera in the Bahamas was 110 miles long and its width ranged between 2 and 12 miles. Heath's misfortunes, caused by his loyalty to the King, gave Sayle an opportunity to exploit the information which he had obtained about Eleuthera. Sayle had come out in strong support of the Parliament in Bermuda against the Royalists. It was therefore relatively easy for him to obtain, through the offices of the Earl of Warwick, who was Governor in Chief of all American plantations, a charter entitling him to settle Eleuthera in 1646. Warwick was at that time the effective ruler of all English settlements overseas and for nearly a decade he remained so after his unique office was created in 1643. It is known that Warwick's principal privateer, Captain Jackson, the man who kept the Spanish Indies in an uproar for three years, had stopped at Bermuda in the autumn of 1644 and it is possible that Sayle spoke with him about his plans.

Sayle's shipwreck off the northern shores of Eleuthera in 1646 made him realise the difficulties and costs of establishing settlements on remote islands whose seas had not been adequately charted. And so the company of Eleutherian Adventurers was formed in London in order to obtain enough capital to finance a permanent settlement and to gather all information possible from persons with experience of other overseas plantations. The Puritans had not been too successful with the theocracies which they had transplanted to Massachusetts and to Providence Island off the Mosquito Coast. Accordingly, articles of the Adventurers stipulated that 'no notice would be taken on Eleuthera of any man for his difference in judgment in matters of religion'. Having scotched the export of religious dissensions to their island the Adventurers prudently drew up articles which restricted participation in the venture to one hundred individuals, each of whom had to make a financial contribution of £100 to the Company. These first hundred Adventurers were designated as the Senate which would have to elect a governor and a council on Eleuthera at the end of three years. As in Bermuda, representation of the company's interests was carefully reserved for decision by the principal shareholders as founding members of the company.

These founding members were each to get 2000 acres of land on Eleuthera and complete possession of all other islands which were to be reserved and laid out for their benefit. The Senate or First Hundred Settlers were instead to receive 300 acres of land, which would be laid out for them and their heirs forever. Christian servants would only be given lands on completion of their periods of indenture; when each would be given 25 acres.

Sayle's original title to Eleuthera was amended in the articles of the company which had been registered in London during the second week of July 1648. The adjacent islands were included at the same time. The articles called the main island which the Adventurers intended to settle, Eleutheria and referred to it as the 'former island of Bahama'. The Spaniards instead knew it as Cigateo when Indians lived there. The articles suggest that the Adventurers still expected to find Indians on the island. They clearly stated that 'no inhabitants of the plantations shall in their converse with any of the natives of any of these parts offer them any wrong, violence or incivility whatsoever; but shall deal with them with all justice and sweetness so far as may stand with their own safety, thereby to work in them a good opinion of love unto the ways and knowledge of God, which everyone shall endeavour to hold forth and communicate unto them in the best manner that they can'. An even loftier expression of goodwill to the original Indian inhabitants of the islands was clearly designed to show the new Puritan arrivals in a very favourable light when contrasted with the Spanish Catholic imperialists. 'Indians taken and sold at some of the Caribbee islands' would be 'sought out, redeemed and afterwards returned to the places from which they were taken'.

Unfortunately, as it turned out, the grand 'Eleutherian' adventure did not really get off the ground and developments in the Bahamas could not compete with the Great Western Design which Cromwell was planning as an extension of Captain Jackson's preliminary privateering expedition against vulnerable Spanish American possessions during the years 1642–44.

In the years immediately following upon the capture of Jamaica from the Spaniards in 1655 Sayle was in London promoting other trading ventures to the East Caribbean as well as to the Bahamas, but he had returned to Bermuda before 1658 when he was reappointed governor there. He seems to have made use of his position in Bermuda to recruit new settlers for Eleuthera. He was later charged with endeavouring to break up the older (Bermudan) colony in favour of Eleuthera. The condition of settlers on Eleuthera attracted governmental attention in England during these years. An order of Council of State dated 16 December 1656 commanded that a letter should be written to the Commander in Chief at Jamaica requesting him to invite about 60 persons then known to be resident on Eleuthera to go to Jamaica or alternatively to be sent back to England. This order is plain enough evidence that the settlement on Eleuthera had not gone according to plan. Sayle continued to be governor in Bermuda until two years after the restoration of Charles II to the throne of England.

It was during the 'sixties that Sayle's island, presumably one of the 'adjacent islands' mentioned in the articles of the Eleutherian Adventurers, was settled. This island, which soon became known as New Providence, had at least 250 settlers by the year 1668, when an appeal was made to Jamaica's Governor Modyford on behalf of their 'elected' governor John Wentworth. Jamaica's governor obliged the petitioners by issuing a commission and instructions to Wentworth, but the brothers Hugh and John Darrell took exception to Modyford's intervention and wrote out instead an attractive prospectus which they sent over to Lord Ashley in England with the suggestion that he, as one of the proprietors of a new grant of the Carolinas made by Charles II, might like to obtain a grant of the Bahamas. The suggestion bore fruit and on 1 November 1670 Charles II granted the islands of the Bahamas to six of the Lords Proprietors of Carolina, namely the Duke of Albermarle, the Earl of Craven, Lord Berkley, Lord Ashley, Sir George Carteret, and Sir Peter Colleton. With this grant the first real chapter in the history of the Bahamas as an extension of Britain overseas was opened. Everything before this date is introduction. The new grant completely ignored the Royal gift to Attorney General Heath and invalidated the Rump Parliament Act of 1649 on behalf of the Adventurers. William Sayle's role in the new development is none too clear, but he was not entirely overlooked for the proprietors of the Carolinas chose him in 1670 to govern their small settlement at Charles Town which was to develop much later into the principal city of South Carolina. Carolina and not the Bahamas was to be Sayle's final reward for organising the Adventurers and persuading so many Bermudans to become the first European pioneer settlers of the low-sea islands.

When the Proprietors took over the Bahamas less than 200 persons were living on Eleuthera. Nearly 50 years later conditions had scarcely improved. The articles drawn up by Sayle and his associates remain the most remarkable feature of the whole Eleutherian adventure, which may rightly be considered to have failed absolutely. An observer writing in 1714 on the condition of the islands could account only for a maximum number of 200 families who were then scattered around the archipelago. They lived, he said, on the proceeds of fishing, farming or piracy, 'without any face or form of government, every man doing what's right in his own eyes'.

Eleuthera's land area of 200 square miles is concentrated mostly in the north and south of the island. Its long thin body line seldom exceeds two miles in width.

Most of the developments which attract the notice of today's visitors on Eleuthera took place after the end of World War II They included restructuring of roads, repairs and repainting of houses, construction of new buildings, multi-million dollar resort complexes, airports and services. Modern Eleuthera is a product of the technological age. It could not develop gradually by employment of its own storage of skills, but had to import them from outside. This transformation is nowhere more apparent than at Powell Point where even temporary accommodations for workers were brought in from the United States and assembled on site.

The best-known island dependencies of Eleuthera are located on either side of the northern mainland. Current island, where a great variety of straw goods are made for sale in Nassau, is long and slim and is mainly covered by scrub and palm trees. Current Cut separates it from the Current settlement, which is conspicuous for its tall casuarinas and neat wooden houses. Houses there attracted the attention of a visitor as long ago as 1888. He called them 'above the average', but observed that the 'poorest coloured' people were living 'in wretched huts made of palmetto thatch'. There was at the time flourishing export of coconuts, oranges, limes and bananas to the United States. The people of the Current believe that the first settlement was made there by survivors from the shipwreck off Ridley Head in 1646. They are supposed to have gone there after an initial period of 'residence' in Preacher's Cave, which modern anthropologists assert was used as a burial ground by the Lucayans of pre-Columbian times.

The Current is very popular today with sea-going families who make good use of the facilities available at the Current Club, which is about nine miles by road from North Eleuthera's small airport.

The Bluff, a coastal settlement to the west of the airstrip, is called by Eleutherans the 'heartland' of agriculture. The farmers of the Bluff are descended from liberated African slaves who early developed the spirit of enterprise. Until the United States imposed restrictive tariffs in the late nineteenth century the farmers of the Bluff found profitable outlets for their pineapples and other fruit crops in Baltimore, Wilmington, Brunswick and other towns on the mainland of America.

Five miles across the water north of the Bluff, is the village and harbour of Spanish Wells on St George's Cay. It derives its name from the reputation which the wells of olden times enjoyed with visiting Spanish sailors, who considered them as Spanish by right of discovery. The water at Spanish Wells today is pumped two miles across the seabed by pipes from the mainland of Eleuthera. Until recent years Spanish Wells was a white enclave. The people who live there now enjoy high reputations as fishermen and market gardeners. Pride in their loyalist ancestors is reflected in their gaily painted small houses and neat garden plots. The village was not always a showplace. In 1812 it was sacked and plundered by American sailors during their second war against Great Britain.

Lloyds resort is a centre for scuba divers and offers other

facilities. Yachts are looked after at Echo Marina, Sawyers Marina and Roberts Harbour Club. Tennis is one of the shore activities on Spanish Wells, which is also the home of the Bahamian broad-rimmed hat.

Brilanders or Harbour Islanders are easily persuaded that their island is the most favoured of the archipelago. Discriminating winter visitors share this view and quite a number have bought colonial type wooden homes in Dunmore Town or have built 'Bay' houses along the pink strand of the Atlantic coastline. According to an American attorney-at-law, who has explored most of the populated islands, there is none to compare with Harbour Island. It is a very small island on which a seven-mile walk would bring you back to your point of departure. Yet within this small land area live more than 3000 people. The mainland is less than 30 minutes away by ferry and from the ferry dock it is only ten minutes' drive to North Eleuthera's airport. Yet the intervening sea lake between big island and small island gives the Brilanders a sensation of complete separation from the pulse of Bahamian enterprise. The Brilanders are within the Bahamas, but their pace of living is controlled by themselves. I was given an early lesson by the taxi-driver who answered to the name of Mr Cool, although his real name is Major. 'Everybody calls me Mr Cool', he told me, 'because I never worry about anything'. And once you are on Harbour island the sane thing *is* to take it cool and to let surplus energies find outlets in underwater exploration, yachting, sailing, swimming, playing tennis or walking. There really is not a great deal more to do except sleep, relax, read or enjoy the simple pleasures. I can think of nowhere better to do any of these things than at Romora Bay Club, which is managed jointly by an American and his English-born wife. They have stamped their personalities upon a resort which is ideally suited to those who want to enjoy life in a natural setting while surrounded by basic comforts. There may be places elsewhere in the Bahamas or the Caribbean which compare with Romora Bay Club, but I cannot think of a single one. It is so right for an Harbour Island hotel that I would be disappointed if I had to stay anywhere else. Yet there are a number of hotels with deservedly high reputations. Where else would I find a friendly Labrador bitch to show me the way to the Atlantic beach and to stay with me for as long as I wanted? Or where else could I enjoy an ice-cold beer in a bar with a Greek donkey for companion? These essentially rustic pleasures help to give a holiday resort something of the atmosphere of a country hotel and are doubly worthwhile when the food and wine compare favourably with the best obtainable anywhere in large cities.

Oldmixon in the early decades of the eighteenth century recorded that Harbour Island got its name from the goodness of its harbour. At the time there were 20 houses on the island. For most of the century more families lived on Harbour island than on Eleuthera and in 1783 Andrew Deveaux was able to recruit a number of 'Brilanders' for his expedition against the Spaniards who had held Nassau for a year. This service to the British throne was suitably rewarded by the Crown when the people of Harbour Island were granted rights to farm lands on North Eleuthera. Some years later the Governor and Commander in Chief of the Bahamas, the Earl of Dunmore, selected Harbour Island as a place of summer residence. From that day onward the Brilanders have had little reason to doubt that what was good enough for the Earl was good enough for themselves. It would have been remarkable if under the circumstances the established white families of Harbour Island had not acquired a sense of superiority which has persisted to the present day. Despite the tendency for the white Brilanders to dwell in isolated 'ivory towers' the average black Brilander seems relatively content with his lot and is particularly well disposed to visitors.

The marked placidity of life on Harbour Island was rudely shattered by a hurricane in 1928. One of the 'sights' it left behind is an upturned tamarind tree which gives useful shade in Willie's, the chief restaurant of the town outside the hotel circuit. The Anglican churchbell rings with a cracked note, but is easily audible from the sea. Brilanders still remember when the evening curfew was sounded by a policeman who rang a bell outside the post office at nine every evening.

The Commissioner of Harbour Island lives in a Colonial-style wooden mansion not far from the landing pier. His presence makes the island a port of entry for the Bahamas. A private airstrip (1300 feet) is located south of Dunmore Town, but the savour of a Briland holiday requires approach by the ferry boat the motion of which is attuned to the slow pace of living ashore.

After the experience of the narrow land area of Harbour Island Eleuthera's main highway of nearly 100 miles seems very long indeed. An official publication says that a good road runs the entire length of the island, but it is as well to be prepared for quite large pot-holes on certain stretches. Between Hatchet Bay and Governor's Harbour local residents can maintain speed only because they are skilled 'navigators'. The Glass Window near North Eleuthera's airport used to be a sight of great beauty when the natural arch joined together rocks which had been eroded into the shape of a window by the action of waves through the centuries. During the hurricane the natural arch was broken. Today a modern bridge spans the gulf and permits the passage of motor vehicles from North to Central and South Eleuthera.

Hatchet Bay Harbour was a salt-water lake until a 90-foot channel was cut after the end of World War 1 by an Englishman, George Benson, who wanted the coral stone as building material. Today the harbour is a favourite resort for vessels in the hurricane season. Hatchet Bay developed as headquarters of the farming enterprise started by Austin Levy of Harrisville in 1927. For years much of the milk and poultry consumed in the Bahamas originated on 2500 acres of the Hatchet Bay Plantation, but in 1973 there were no more herds and the silos and grasslands showed signs of neglect. According to my taxi-driver, who knows Eleuthera better than most living persons, wild dogs roam the fields and discourage the keeping of livestock. The Yacht Club at Hatchet Bay caters to visiting yachtsmen and there are some attractive houses in the village.

Not far from the fishing village of James Cistern behind Pelican Cay the United States Air Force has a missile tracking station and its own airstrip. The missile base is one of a series which stretch from Florida to Ascension Island. The Cliffs north of the village provide spectacular views of the Atlantic. Seven miles to the south is Governors Harbour, one of the oldest and most picturesque of settlements in the Bahamas. There is a tradition that Cupid's Cay (which is now connected by a causeway to the town) was selected by early settlers, who moved down from the Current. Another tradition tells how these settlers, in gratitude for aid received from Boston Puritans, shipped ten tons of braziletto wood to that city from the proceeds of which a donation was given to Harvard College. The tradition is quite credible because the Puritans of America maintained close contact in the seventeenth century with Puritans on other overseas plantations. The sight of Cupid's Cay from the hill overlooking Governor's Harbour is arresting. It is not surprising that Winslow Homer successfully portrayed its appeal in several paintings. Governor's Harbour is served by a modern airport with daily flights to Nassau. It has a bank, resident doctor and dentist and is close to a number of modern beach clubs.

Behind the High Bluff facing Levy island to the north of Governor's Harbour is the Eleuthera Marine and Sports company, a joint apartment and service enterprise founded by New Zealander David Mitchell.

Tarpum Bay in the south has a picturesque church and several interesting old wooden houses. A turreted house on the outskirts belongs to painter Gordon Macmillan-Hughes, whose works are displayed in the village's art gallery. The life style of Tarpum Bay is happily caught in a large mural which adorns the main club room of Cotton Bay Club. In earlier days pineapples were shipped in quantity from this little port which today sleeps in the sun, as though every day were Sunday. The east coast of Eleuthera is particularly attractive between Savannah Sound, north of Tarpum Bay and the Cotton Bay Club, south of Rock Sound. A beach club development on Windermere island in the Atlantic is made accessible by a bridge from the mainland.

A cluster of four attractive Atlantic-facing resorts are managed by Franz Gross, one of the many dedicated hoteliers who have given the Out-islands of the Bahamas reputations for excellent service, food and reliability. Two of the four, Eleuthera Beach Inn and Rock Sound Club Beach Cottages on Winding Bay, are near to Tarpum Bay. Rock Sound Club, close to its own modern 7000 foot airport, has direct flights by Pan American to New York and connecting flights through Nassau to other North American and European destinations. Fourteen miles away at Cotton Bay is Robert Trent Jones' 18-hole golf course which offers splendid views of the Atlantic coastline and has fairways bordered by coconut palms, casuarinas, and other shade giving trees. Many of the world's best golfers have played on this course and many of the world's most famous men and women have visited Rock Sound Club. The beach cottages on Cotton Bay are open all the year round. Food is excellent and varied. Lobsters are of superlative quality. Several private houses have been built near the beach and around Cotton Bay blending harmoniously against a green covered landscape that merges into a promontory running southward to Eleuthera point. At Rock Sound, New Portsmouth is headquarters for Eleuthera South Island Resorts. There are well stocked grocery and food stores, bank, post office and maintenance shops. There is also a government dock.

Powell Point, at the extreme northern tip of South Eleuthera, has a modern American development known as the Cape Eleuthera resort colony. Millions of dollars were spent on reclaiming beaches, building causeways, landscaping an 18-hole golf course, putting in roads, water, sewage and electrical power. A marina, which cost one million dollars to construct, has a 400-foot commercial dock and 26 docking slips.

It is not at all easy to convey an overall impression of a boomerang-shaped, thin-bodied island which bulges sideways at its northern and southern ends. The long stretches of road between settlements and their relatively small populations intensify the tendency to individual patterns of behaviour which are characteristic of pioneer communities. This spirit of isolationism is reinforced by the absence of local government at the level of an Eleutheran community. An Out island is regarded as a bailiwick for which a particular politician is responsible to the centre of power in Nassau rather than as a community of people whose elected representative goes to Nassau to ensure that the views of his community triumph over party views. Throughout Eleuthera there is a feeling that no matter what Eleutherans might feel about situations the real decisions will be taken by a majority of politicians with no direct knowledge of their needs. There could be no greater contrast with this status of provincial dependence upon a capital city and the original concept of the first Adventurers that their affairs would be controlled by a Senate elected by themselves.

In this respect Eleuthera is no different from other Out islands, but the occurrence of highly developed resort complexes and the application of modern technologies on Hatchet Bay and Rock

Sound plantations suggest that continuity of progress in the future will require a greater number of residents working together as a community. The major impression which the visitor takes away is of a series of population centres whose levels of social achievement are very uneven. Where the twentieth century has blasted away obstacles in new development areas the situation somehow resembles that of autonomous army, naval or airforce bases operating upon foreign soils but supplied with resources and skills from overseas.

SUMMARY:

Eleuthera and its Islands
Population: Over 3000 on Harbour Island: over 7000 on other islands.
Size: 200 square miles: 110 miles long by 2½ miles wide (average).
Location: About 60 miles east of Nassau.
Airports: North Eleuthera, Governor's Harbour (centre USAF), Rock Sound (South). Daily service.
Ferry Service: To Harbour Island and Spanish Wells.
Ground Transport: Taxis and rental vehicles.
Settlements.
North: Current Island, the Current, Spanish Wells, Harbour Island, The Bogues, Gregory Town, Hatchet Bay.
Centre: James Cistern, US Navy Base, Governor's Harbour, Tarpum Bay.
South: New Portsmouth, Rock Sound, Powell Point, Freetown, Wemyss Bight, Bannerman Town, Millers.
Harbours: Davis Harbour (between Deep Creek and Wemyss Bight), Cape Eleuthera, Rock Sound, Tarpum Bay, Governor's Harbour, Hatchet Bay, Dunmore Town, Spanish Wells, Royal Island, The Current.
Places of Special Interest:
North: Ridley Head, Preacher's Cave (about 18 miles from N. Eleuthera airport), Dunmore Town, Spanish Wells, The Current, The Bluff, The Glass Window (about 10 miles south of N. Eleuthera airport), The Cove (Gregory Town), The Cave (north of

Hatchet Bay), Hatchet Bay Plantation (about 13 miles north of Governor's Harbour Airport), The Cliffs.
Centre: Governor's Harbour, Tarpum Bay.
South: Rock Sound, Cotton Bay, Cape Eleuthera, Bannerman Town, Davis Harbour, Green Castle, Wemyss Bight, Ocean Hole.

SPECIAL NOTES FOR HARBOUR ISLAND.

Telephone Exchange open from 0800 until 1 pm (near Post Office). Reconfirm flight reservations 72 hours before departure. Southern tip of island is privately owned.

8 The Exuma Cays, Long Island, Cat, Little San Salvador, Goat Island, San Salvador, Rum Cay, Conception Island, the Jumentos Cays and Ragged Island

Natural beauty is prodigally displayed throughout the Bahamian archipelago but nowhere is it more concentrated than among the necklace of islets and cays which occupy 90 miles of sea between New Providence and Long Island. There are approximately 365 in a chain which extends in a southeasterly direction from a point about 35 miles from Nassau. On a sunny day earth has nothing to show more fair than the kaleidoscope which the traveller sees through the windows of an aeroplane. Swirling folds of blue, aquamarine, green and crystal clear waters flash by, interrupted occasionally by vistas of tiny beaches, pressed roadways, villas and landlocked harbours. For most of the way the traveller sees patterns under the water of mountains, plains and canals which flow between delicately combed ridges of sand. It is not surprising that 22 miles of this earthly paradise have been reserved as the Exuma Cays Land and Sea Park. The area extends from Wax Cay Cut southwards to Conch Cut. Under by-laws administered by the Bahamas National Trust pollution of lands or waters is forbidden and removal or destruction of plant, animal or marine life is prohibited. Exceptions are made for sports fishermen who use hand lines, hand-held spears or Hawaiian slings. Catches are limited to personal consumption on board cruising vessels. Giant iguanas once flourished in the small cluster of islets collectively known as the Allan Cay Group. They have long since departed. Allan's

Cay Harbour, formerly a popular resort of sponge fishermen, still offers yachtsmen useful anchorage. Highborne Cay, which has some high ground, is two miles long and can be easily identified by yachtsmen approaching the Exumas from Powell Point on Eleuthera. Many years ago the island was farmed extensively. Today it is privately owned, but yachtsmen can avail themselves of facilities which are provided in the main harbour. Norman's Cay further south is only 3½ miles long but has 10 miles of sandy beach. It has a yacht club and a 3000 ft airstrip.

Saddle Cay near the northern end of Norman's Cay is privately owned. Wax Cay, which denotes the northern boundary of the Exuma Cays and Land Park, is also within easy reach by boat. It has sandy beaches and hills rising up to 93 feet. Little Pigeon Cay, a privately owned island, lies at the southern tip of the small archipelago collectively called Pigeon or Shroud Cay. Little Pigeon is the terminal point of the Whit Monday race organised by the Nassau Yacht Squadron.

On Halls Pond Cay there is a service dock and a club (the Exuma Cays Club) which provides refreshment and some services. Little Bell island is located in the waters which run through Conch Cut into the Exuma Sound at the southern boundary of the Land and Sea Park. Fowl Cay, another privately owned island has a 1300 foot airstrip.

Compass Cay, which comprises twin high rising islands separated by a mangrove swamp, is also privately owned. White cliffs at the northeastern end are conspicuous from the sea.

No less than 17 cays, collectively known as Pipe Creek, are spread across the popular cruising grounds which lie between Compass Cay and Staniel Cay. Fuel and supplies may be obtained in Sampson Cay Harbour, where there is a small store. About 100 seafaring, sea-loving people live on Staniel Cay. The Yacht Club presents itself as the ideal headquarters for yachting and sports fishing in the Exumas. Its facilities include a deepwater dock, usual services, complete skin-scuba equipment, water skiing and guided tours to the 'Thunderball' caves. The Club maintains a 2600 foot paved airstrip.

The friendly villagers on Staniel Cay live in neat, well painted homes among flowering shrubs. Visitors are made very welcome at the Royal Entertainer's Lounge while Kenneth's Lounge pro-

23 and 24 (opposite) top: Statue of Queen Victoria and Government Buildings facing Rawson Square, Nassau; bottom: Government House, Nassau

vides local entertainment. Yachtsmen from all over the Exumas meet at Staniel Cay for the August bank holiday picnic at Harvey Cay, where there is a well protected anchorage at the north-western end.

The largest native settlement in the Exumas, other than on Great Exuma, is Black Point at the northern end of Great Guana Cay. At least 300 persons live there. Direct telecommunication services are maintained with Nassau. Facing the southern tip of Great Guana Cay is the settlement on Little Farmer's Cay. Many of the settlers are retired pilots and sea captains. Big Farmer's Cay, which is separated from Great Guana Cay by Farmer's Cay Cut, has some fine beaches, established coconut groves, clusters of casuarinas and hills. Galliot Cut and its cays divide Farmer's Cay from Cave Cay a hilly island with high cliffs, and several caves. A beacon light on Cave Cay has a visibility of seven miles at sea. The island was once cultivated. Thick stone walls and an old ruin still survive around lands once used as pastures.

Rudder Cut Cay has an inland lake and an airstrip. It is priv-ately owned. The privately owned Darby Island and Little Darby island were developed before the last war as cattle farms and planted with thousands of coconut trees. A group of neighbouring cays are registered as bird sanctuaries.

On Barreterre, Kermit's Hilltop restaurant has an open dance floor and a panoramic view of cays and coastlines. The road climbs up past gaily painted hill-side houses. Steventon five miles to the south, is a pretty, coconut-fringed beach-side settlement which has a private clinic.

George Town is a port of entry for the Bahamas. It has a clinic and resident doctor, and an efficient postal service. A 3000 foot airstrip is used by planes connecting with Nassau, Stella Maris and Florida.

After the agreement of August 1940 made with Great Britain, the United States Navy began construction of a seaplane base at George Town. At that time the idea may have been born of developing home sites in the Exumas. Yet George Town did not grow or develop into a large Bahamian city and today there is little sign of American influence except perhaps high prices, American visitors, American yachts and cruisers and some Ameri-can cars. The first impression of George Town's tiny airport is of

25 *(opposite) International Bazaar, Freeport, Grand Bahama*

I

a destination very distant in time from the pace and bustle of Nassau. It is as though a time clock had been mysteriously put back for thirty years. 'Hurry' is a word without a meaning at George Town where everything has to happen eventually if you have the patience to wait. To show impatience would be to invite resentment from people who have no objection to taking money from tourists but who are quite convinced that all tourists like George Town and the Exumas generally because of the plentiful peace they find there. If there is impatience in George Town it is impatience of a system which makes life on Exuma far more expensive than in Nassau because Nassau is an exporting city and George Town a receiving village. Change is desirable if only it means that bread consumed in George Town is baked on the spot and not imported from Nassau. If time does not actually stand still at George Town it moves at very slow speed around the evergreen tree where straw workers present the major industry of the land dwelling islanders. For three days during April the harbour at George Town, which is named Elizabeth after Elizabeth Island, is the setting for the Out Islands Regatta. Stocking island, at the other end of the harbour, is exceptionally beautiful; here some fine houses have been constructed for rich residents. It has relatively high hills, a mile-long ocean beach and several smaller beaches with traditional sea island coconut groves. Peace and Plenty Hotel in George Town has its own beach club on Stocking island. Guests are taken across by boat and can spend many hours collecting sea shells on the ocean beach.

The Government building on the seafront in George Town is a fine example of colonial architecture which still conveys an aura of the authority that once upheld commissioners in outposts of Empire. Every morning the new Bahamian flag is raised on the flagpole outside by a uniformed policeman who performed the same duty with a Union Jack before Bahamian independence was proclaimed in July 1973. Inside in an upper office the resident commissioner still enshrines the principle that George Town is on the periphery of a power structure which is rooted in Nassau. His presence in these lonely corridors of outer power embalms a system more than it charts signs of change in the community where he temporarily resides.

Even more remote from island life seems the small village

church set on a bluff overlooking a lagoon across the way from the Peace and Plenty Hotel. Inscriptions in the graveyard recall not so distant days when men believed in an Empire on which the sun would never set and in a faith especially tailored for the needs of imperial administration in remote outposts. The sun has set and that faith now seeks renewal in other converts, but the church in George Town still stands foursquare to the winds of change, a monument of a past which can never be renewed. On a night of scudding tropical clouds and soft moonbeams I stood in silence wondering how much longer an active Anglican faith could have meaning for people so remote from the country which brought it to birth.

Further south at Rolle Town I met a Baptist minister who was introduced as the Reverend Rolle and presented as the head of the Rolle clan. He was a tall handsome Bahamian past 60. We met in the open air beneath the shade of a sugar apple tree and talked briefly about the needs of the Exuman people. What did a family of eight require to support themselves above the poverty line? His prompt answer was $8000 a year.

Before I left the venerable Rolle at the foot of Rolle Town hill the cicadas were voicing their appreciation of the warm sun. Throughout the islands these transparent-winged shrill-toned insects are known as 'the singers' and their songs are accepted everywhere as indication of hot sunny weather. I had heard these singers in places as remote as Broumana in Lebanon and the Mediterranean isle of Capri. On both occasions they sang monotonously, steadily and with no apparent recognition of the cries of neighbouring cicadas. At Rolle Town instead I heard cicadas singing in several groups of tree choruses separated from each other by an intervening roadway. The effect was remarkably like that produced in dual amplifiers by a stereophonic recording; *the sounds seemed to be alternating from either side of the road as though one chorus of cicadas could hear the other and was responding in turn.* Such a theory conflicts with the suggestion that cicadas are deaf.

The legend which associates the name of Pretty Molly Bay with a beautiful mermaid who sings siren songs from a rock nearby is appropriate, if only because the Bay is startlingly beautiful. I cannot easily explain why I kept on thinking of the *Moon and*

Sixpence all the time I was at Pretty Molly Bay, yet the setting of a 'bay house' among sea grapes and vine covered dunes with clear vistas of islands and translucent sea released a chain of thoughts linked with escapists' paradises. If ever a place was designed as a haven for escapists and maintained with that theme in mind it is surely Pretty Molly Bay. It is on Little Exuma island, a short distance from the point where a small bridge has replaced the ferry and attached the 12-mile-long island of rolling farmlands to Great Exuma. Pretty Molly may never have existed as mermaid or woman, but the bay is formed of pretty islets, pretty coves, pretty waters and pretty sands. And on the other side at Mariah Harbour Cay are more pretty beaches and coves liberally adorned with sea shells.

Little Exuma has three settlements at the Ferry, Forbes Hill and Williams Town. An abandoned salt pond south of Williams Town recalls the role that the Exumas used to play as suppliers of salt in the seventeenth century. The Cotton House claimed as the oldest building in the Exumas is still used as a residence. It was the central administrative headquarters of a 970 acre cotton plantation when it was constructed in the eighteenth century by Roger Kelsall.

Hog Cay beyond Little Exuma is a well cultivated island and has a 2000 foot airstrip. The remains of a lookout tower and an ancient cannon bring to mind its role in earlier days as an advanced outpost for the ships which made use of Elizabeth Harbour.

Long Island

Cape Santa Maria, the northernmost point on Long Island, lies 27 miles northeast of George Town on Great Exuma. A private airstrip serves the Cape Santa Maria club. Yuma, the Arawak name for Long Island, was called Fernandina by Christopher Columbus in honour of the Spanish King who financed his voyage of discovery. In his diary on 16 October 1492 Columbus noted that Fernandina was exceeding large and 'on it or near it there is a mine of gold'. He said that the islanders knew how to trade in bartering cotton or other little things and observed that cotton cloth was worn there 'like mantles'. The women also wore 'in front a small piece of cotton stuff which scarcely covers what decency requires'. Columbus was puzzled by trees which apparently had branches of many different kinds growing out of a single trunk; for instance one branch had leaves like those of cane and another like those of mastic. He was also impressed by the fish which were 'so different from ours that it is a wonder. Some look like cocks of the finest colours in the world, blue, yellow, red and all colours the other variegated in a thousand fashions'. He records the presence of whales in the sea near the island, but found no other wild life except parrots and lizards. A young man told him that he had seen a large snake and sailors reported the presence of non-barking dogs. Near the northwest of the island he found a natural harbour with an island at the entrance.

Columbus received a warm welcome at Fernandina because he had literally picked up a Lucayan travelling in a canoe from the island which he called Santa Maria. He took the man and his boat on board his own vessel and shortly after arrival was rewarded by a group of welcoming Lucayans who helped him find water and to fill up the containers which he had brought ashore. It was on the second day of his stay on Long Island that Columbus went for a walk underneath trees that were the 'most beautiful he had ever seen'. He found the vegetation abundant and as fresh as May in Andalusia although the trees were as different from Spain's as night from day as also were the fruits, the grass, the stones and everything else. Later Columbus was told by sailors who went in search of water that they had visited the dwellings of Lucayans and found them well swept and clean. The Lucayans on Long Island lived in villages in groups of between 12 and 15 tent-like buildings. Their 'beds', which were hammocks, resembled nets made from cotton. It began to rain heavily between midnight and dawn and Columbus noted that ever since his arrival in the Indies it rained more or less every day. He concludes his entry for 17 October by asking their Highnesses to believe that the country is the most fertile, temperate and good to be found in the world. Columbus saw these new islands through rose-tinted glasses. He called them collectively 'Le Principesse'. Oviedo said this was because they were the 'beginnings' of the sight he was getting of 'these Indies'. To his excited mind they might well have looked like 'Princesses'.

Today a long road runs between Stella Maris in the north and Clarence Town in the south. It is kept in good repair and at intervals passes through settlements which are easily distinguished by ultra-modern churches. Some farms near the highway are enclosed by walls of heaped stones. The fields are planted with a variety of fruit trees (bananas, coconuts, sugar, apples, mangoes, grapefruit, chili plums, avocados) and there are occasional clusters of pigeon peas and sugar canes. The long distances between settlements on Long Island, where the sea is never more than five miles distant, emphasise the importance of movement by sea in the earlier patterns of development.

The approach to Clarence Town from the rolling northern highway is a strange experience. As if from nowhere two imposing European-style churches suddenly appear on opposing cupped hilltops as though dropped ready made from the sky. Both churches were designed by the Anglican-Catholic priest architect Father Jerome, who left many other examples of temples in other islands of the Bahamas. Strangely the church of St Paul's built in his days as an Anglican priest has more Catholic atmosphere because of a screen suggestive of Papal authority than does the cheap-looking modern altar of his St Peter's Catholic church. The exterior of St Peter's, however, is most impressive because of the wide stone steps that lead down a sloping hill to wooden houses which recall life styles of earlier centuries. Despite the mosquitoes which sting and sing energetically at nightfall the 65-mile journey from Stella Maris to Clarence Town is worthwhile if only to see the remarkable twin churches which proclaim the twin faiths of Father Jerome, Anglican and Catholic priest.

The Commissioner for Long Island has a modern office near the dock in Clarence Town. Several stores supply the needs of over 200 persons and a resident nurse is in charge of the clinic. South of Clarence Town harbour there are settlements at Dunmore, Hard Bargain, Molly Well, Roses and Mortimers. To the west of these settlements are salt flats controlled by the Diamond Crystal Salt Company.

Long Island's 'pot hole' farming is mainly conducted by families who live in communities at Buckley's, Cartwright Landing and Mangrove Bush. Pineapples, mangoes, tomatoes, onions, cabbages and limes are their favourite crops. These communities live close to the large settlement at Deadman's Cay which has direct air connections with Nassau, and a large modern store. In recent years there has been a revival of the sponge industry at Salt Pond a few miles north of Deadman's Cay. Yachtsmen are very welcome at Salt Pond which has a small inn near McKie's dock. The Long Island Regatta is held there every year in May. Metered fuel and gasoline are obtainable at the government dock which also has facilities for repairs.

One of the sights of Simms, the settlement closest to the new development at Stella Maris, is a stoutly built stone structure with the inscription 'Her Majesty's Prison'. According to local report there have been no prisoners there for a very long time. Other features of this farming and fishing community are stone walls and casuarina shaded houses. Simms has a clinic and resident nurse and several small stores. In recent years there has been a revival of sponge fishing. The casuarina-shaded Deale's beach on the way to Simms is popular with residents at the Stella Maris Inn and is ideal for horse-back riding.

Development of Stella Maris Estates on Long Island was started by Johann and Hilde Aufochs in 1964. By the end of 1972 over $6.5 million had been spent on construction of many miles of good roads, a 4250 foot airstrip, a harbour and marina, a modern shopping centre, tennis courts and club house and other amenities. German and other investors provided most of the capital for the development and the Stella Maris Inn, a hilltop complex of clubhouse and cottages running down to the sea is under German management. Fresh water is pumped from 50 wells by power supplied by the Stella Maris Water Power and Lighting Company. Stella Maris Estates allotted 2500 acres of land for sale to individuals and made provision for an 18-hole golf course and a hotel that 'blends with the natural beauty of the island'. Meanwhile the Stella Maris Inn fulfils the role of social centre for a community of residents and visitors and enjoys a reputation for diving facilities which puts it among the top five resorts of the Caribbean and Bahamas. Jorge Friese, owner of the Stella Maris, is not only a first-class skin diver and scuba guide, but has an instructor's rating from the Barakuda Klub, West Germany's large diver certification agency. Stella Maris offers at least 25 different diving areas, but eight of them are especially recommended.

Tony's Reef, nine miles north of the marina on the west side of Long Island, runs parallel to the shore for approximately three quarters of a mile. Visibility is up to 100 feet at water depths between 30 and 35 feet. Spearfishing is prohibited, so fish are plentiful and friendly. Photographers can capture splendid views of fish grazing among colourful sea plumes and corals.

Spearfishing is not allowed at Harry's Heads, a group of six coral heads not far from Tony's Reef. The heads are between 100 and 200 feet apart and are alive with corals, sea fans, anemones, sponges and other forms of marine life.

At Barracuda Heads, not more than two miles distant from Harry's Heads, spearfishing is permitted with Hawaiian slings. Hunters have to be very quick if they want to preserve their catch from the barracudas who give their name to the 25 heads which teem with crevices and archways inhabited by tiny fish. About one mile off Columbus Point, the northernmost tip of Long Island, is Heidi's Reef, named after a lady diver from Nuremberg. Very large fish take shelter in the crevices of this reef below the 50 feet initial drop which slopes steeply downwards for another 40 feet. At this point fish move from the sheltered Exuma Sound into the open Atlantic.

Big Reef, which begins seven miles west of the marina, is an 18 mile coral reef running from Long Island to the lower Exumas. Depths on the outside go to 40 feet and average 25 feet on the inside. Deep channels divide the reef at intervals. The reef is popular with island fishermen who make regular catches of grouper, snapper, rock fish and other Bahamian delicacies.

About five miles north of the Stella Maris Inn only 50 yards from the beach is House Reef, which slopes down gradually from 10 to 40 feet. It is protected by a barrier reef from swells and is very suitable for snorkeling and scuba diving. Coral Gardens on the east side of the island, a mile north of Stella Maris Inn has a forest of antler coral. The reef begins about 200 yards from shore and runs out for another 150 yards at depths between 12 and 20 feet. Visibility is not good at times of ocean swells.

A Blue Hole on the east of Long Island is situated 50 miles south of Stella Maris. The water surrounding the hole is only two feet deep but the hole, which has an initial diameter of 200 feet has been sounded to a depth of 900 feet. The 'walls' are bell shaped and the diameter decreases with depth. Visibility is about 100 feet.

An all-day boat trip from Long Island takes divers to and from Conception Island, 14 miles northeast of the northern tip of Long Island. Departures from the marina are as early as three or four in the morning. At least 30 ships have been wrecked off Conception and it is quite easy to drop anchor on one of them. Green and hawksbill turtles frequent the area. Depths range between 35 and 70 feet. Stella Maris Inn also arranges day cruises to Rum Cay, where the British warship *Ocean Conqueror* ran aground on a reef in 1862 and sank with 101 cannons on board. Stella Maris Inn offers divers package tours at reduced rates between April 1st and December 20th, which is the best time of the year for diving. The tropic of Cancer passes through Simms on Long Island. Stella Maris airport for this reason may be regarded as a half way staging post for flyers commuting between Nassau and the southern-most island of Inagua. While I was at the Inn in September 1973, a Canadian pilot flew almost daily to neighbouring islands like Cat, San Salvador, Inagua and occasionally to Haiti. He had flown over every square mile of the Bahamas and considered that the best fishing grounds were to be found in the waters between Crooked Island and Acklins.

The communications tower which sits above the roof of Stella Maris Inn and which was being painted by an Abaconian on the day of my arrival, marks the hub of the communication system which keeps Stella Maris in touch with the world outside. I was not the least surprised to hear the young Bahamian lady on duty call up her brother, a pilot of Bahamasair to check the exact time of arrival of the plane which was to take me back to Nassau. The tradition of mutual assistance which goes back to Columbus' arrival in October 1492 is still entrenched on Long Island at Stella Maris. Incidentally it was the only hotel in the Bahamas where I found a plate of fresh fruit in my room.

Cat Island is unique in the Bahamas for hills which reach over 200 feet at several points. Only about 48 miles long and between one and four miles wide it resembles an unwieldy mechanical claw in shape with a neck far more like a giraffe's than a cat's.

Some Bahamians are still convinced that Cat, not Watling's island was the first land sighted by Columbus but the weight of historical opinion is against them. There are less than 3000 residents of Cat Island of whom more than 1100 attend schools in 14 settlements.

Cat Island is the homeland of the Poitiers. Sidney is still spoken of as 'the local boy who made good'. It is also the final resting place of the church-building Anglican priest who died in the Catholic faith. In 1948 he built a simple church in the Bight and at the summit of Mount Alvernia formerly known as Como Hill his body rests in a cave beneath the Hermitage he erected 204 feet above sea level. Stations of the Cross are carved in rock along the path leading to the summit of the hill. An American priest who took over the Hermitage invites visitors to strike a gong before beginning the climb above.

Cat Island saw days of prosperity when American loyalists exploited the relatively rich soils, but the ruins of old plantation houses still bear silent witness to longer periods of decay. Horses and cattle were once raised extensively on Port Howe estate on the south of the island where the land is 14 miles wide. Valuable wood like madeira, mahogany, braziletto, lignum vitae and several varieties of palm also flourished in the east coast. The main settlement areas for the private small farmers extend for 30 miles between Bluff and New Bight, where the commissioner has a residence. Farming is still the major occupation of the islanders who grow tomatoes, pineapples, peas, bananas, watermelon and other crops for export to Nassau. Old Bight near Armbristers Creek is especially famous for its sugarloaf pineapples. They are plentiful in May and June. There is a very beautiful unspoilt beach which runs for three miles from Old Bight. Hawks Nest Fishing and Yacht Club is a convenient stopover centre for yachts returning to Nassau from the George Town Regatta. A small airstrip is near the club for the use of charter or private aircraft. Other arrivals by air are met at New Bight airport 40 minutes drive from the club.

Cutlass Bay Club, which lies half way between Hawksnest Creek and Columbus Point in the toe of Cat Island, is built on 'stilts' on the side of a sloping hill which gives exciting views of bright blue Bahamian sea.

The Fernandez Bay Club which lies a few miles north of New

Bight is advertised as the 'world's largest thatch roof resort with a million hand-tied palm leaves'. Cat islanders were long famous for their thatched roofs made of palm leaves which had an average life of between ten and twelve years. The commissioner for the north end of Cat Island has his headquarters at Arthur's Town, where there is a telephone station, a resident nurse and an airport.

The majority of Cat Islanders use horses for transport, but cars or trucks are available for rental at most of the major settlements.

Little San Salvador. Little San Salvador, also known as Little Island or Little Cat Island lies 12 miles west of Alligator Point near Pigeon Cay and 9 miles east-south-east of Eleuthera Point. It is about 5 miles long and a little more than a mile wide. There is a large lagoon where bonefish are sometimes hunted. The island is relatively high and has high rocky ridges in the west covered by shrubs and sago palms. There are coconut groves along the shore. Above the lake are ruins of houses once inhabited by people from Cat Island. Sapodillas and mango trees and wild fowl suggest that farming has not entirely died out on the island. Goat Cay to the north of Little San Salvador is fittingly described as a paradise for nature lovers. Hundreds of seabirds nest there between mid-April and mid-July, doves coo loudly in the branches of sea grape trees and curly-tailed lizards preen themselves in the sun. Explorers may find, however that this animal paradise is protected too fiercely by unfriendly prickly cacti.

To the East of Goat is a chain of islands known collectively as Long Rock.

San Salvador. Guanahani, which Columbus dedicated to Christ the Saviour (San Salvador) on 12 October 1492, is 12 miles long and six miles wide. Much of the interior is covered by lakes, Great Lake being nearly 10 miles long and two miles wide at one part. The hill known as Mount Kerr is 140 feet above sea level. Columbus was not greatly impressed by its height. His description of San Salvador is of an island reasonably large and flat without any mountain, profusely covered with green trees, rich in water and with a large lagoon in the middle. 'Everything is so green that it is a pleasure to look at'. Besides people the island contained no other living things except parrots. All the people Columbus saw were as naked as their mothers bore them. He did not see any one older than 30 years. Everyone was well built and good looking. Their hair was as thick as the tufts of a horse's tail trimmed in front to reach the eyebrows but trailing behind in long queues. Some were painted with grey, others with white, red and other colours. Some were painted in the face, others all over their body or around the eyes and nose. They had very large beautiful eyes and large foreheads and heads. They were the same colour as the Canary islanders. From the quantity of cotton he saw Columbus concluded that it was grown on the island.

When Columbus understood from the Lucayans that there were enemies who frequently came to attack from the northwest he decided to sail in a south-westerly direction in search of gold and precious stones. As he coasted San Salvador in the direction of north-north-east on the morning of Sunday 14th October an old man came on board and invited all the men and women within range of his voice to 'come and see the men who had fallen from heaven, bring them food and drink'. Despite entreaties Columbus refused to go in near the land because of the low shoals running along the island. It is generally believed that Columbus was referring to Graham Harbour at the north-east corner of San Salvador when he said 'it could hold all the ships in Christendom'. Discovery Day is celebrated each year in Graham Harbour by local smack boats which race for trophies. Along the three-mile sandy beach of Long Bay south of Cockburn Town where the Commissioner lives two monuments record Columbus' first landing on San Salvador. One is a simple stone cross, the other a three-tier brazier erected by the Mexico Olympic Games Committee to record the passage of the Olympic flame from Athens on its way to Mexico City in the New World. In 1891 the *Chicago Herald* was responsible for erecting a monument on a high bluff looking down on a reef studded East Coast to commemorate that paper's conclusion as to the spot where Columbus was most likely to have come ashore. Until the mid-twenties of this century San Salvador was known throughout the Bahamas as Watling's Island after a buccaneer who was supposed to have made his headquarters in a castle at Sandy Point in the south-west. Some historians claim that the castle was the ruins of a Loyalist plantation. G. J. H. Northcroft, whose *Sketches of Summerland* was written in 1899, notes that Watling's Island was dedicated to St Christopher when the Bahamas Parochial Act of 1802 referred to Cat Island as 'the island of San Salvador commonly called Cat Island'.

Northcroft also referred to an abundance of lignum vitae on San Salvador and to the export of horses to Jamaica. These horses were descended from stallions imported from England by the managers of Port Howe Estate on Cat Island. Cat Island at the turn of the century had a much larger population (4648) than today. In September 1968 the San Salvador Teachers' College was opened to provide a three year course for subordinate assistant and uncertificated teachers who could not be trained at the Bahamas Teacher College in Nassau. Examinations are moderated by the University of the West Indies. The College is residential and can accommodate 170 student teachers in buildings of the former United States Air Force base located north of the airstrip near Cockburn Town, which has telecommunications and a resident nurse and clinic. Between the town and the airport is Riding Rock Inn. Visitors to the museum at Polaris which is by the sea a mile north of the Teachers' College, are advised to make prior arrangements with the caretaker who lives in Cockburn Town. Artifacts are assembled in the Columbus Museum which was started by Mrs Fred Melvin.

Rum Cay. San Salvador lies 173 nautical miles south-east of Nassau and less than 50 miles distant from the southern heel of Cat Island. Rum Cay lies 20 miles to the south west of San Salvador and 20 miles east of Cape Santa Maria on Long Island. It is 12 miles long and about seven miles wide in average. Until 1908 salt was exported by Rum Cay to Nova Scotia. Later, pineapple growing and cattle raising were introduced, but less than one hundred persons live on Rum Cay today, mostly at Port Nelson on the south coast. Columbus named Rum Cay after the Conception of Saint Mary, mother of Jesus and made a brief stop there in search of gold. All that he found ashore were a large number of naked people of the same race and quality as those on San Salvador. In modern times Rum Cay has been described as the 'sleeping beauty' of the Bahamas, because of its rolling hills and old ruins. Some of the hills rise to a height of 160 feet. The name of Rum Cay is associated with the wreck of a rum laden ship near its shores.

The Commissioner of San Salvador has responsibility for Rum Cay. Port Nelson, the chief village, is distinguished by groves of casuarinas and coconut trees. St George's Bay below Cottonfield Point has beautiful beaches. Kay's Bar in Port Nelson offers sea food dinners and the Rum Cay Club and Villas are being developed for visitors. A 2500 foot airstrip is available for flying guests. Duck hunting, horse riding and seasports are some of the island's attractions.

Conception Island. Conception Island, which lies 23 miles south-east of Cat Island and 14 miles north-east of Cape Santa Maria, Long Island rises to a height of 90 feet, although it is only 2¾ miles long and no more than 2 miles wide. Booby Cay, one of a series of cays and rocks on the east coast, rises to a height of 130 feet. There is a light tower on a high hill along the west coast of Conception.

Jumentos Reefs and Cays run in a crescent shaped chain over 110 miles along the south-east side of the Great Bahama Barrier. They stretch from Little Water Cay west of Long Island to Little Ragged Island west of Acklins Island in the South Bahamas.

Water Cay probably gets its name from the fact that the sea washes over it in bad weather. Its white cliffs are in the centre. The waters of the chain are usually stormy in the months of winter.

Flamingo Cay south of Water Cay has a lighthouse with flashes visible for 8 miles. It is relatively well covered with trees and has good beaches. South of Flamingo Cay between Man of War channel and Nurse Cay channel are good fishing grounds extending between 16 miles of rocks and cays.

Duncan Town on Great Ragged Island has two schools with over 100 pupils on the rolls. The inhabitants of this settlement on a windswept remote barren island of five square miles scratch their living from the sea and farming on neighbouring cays. Salt for local use is made locally and some straw work is exported to Nassau. A commissioner is resident at Duncan Town, which has direct telephone communications with Nassau. There is a good landlocked harbour. Hog Cay across the harbour is a very attractive, fertile, well-wooded island. Although well off the beaten track of most visitors the Jumentos Reefs and Cays are regarded by enthusiastic yachtsmen as equally deserving of the superlative adjectives more frequently used to describe the kaleidoscope of colours seen by travellers through the Exuma Cays.

SUMMARY :

The Exuma Cays
100 mile arc of more than 350 islands and cays.
Size of Great and Little Exuma : 130 square miles.
Location : Northern tip of chain 35 miles south-south-east of Nassau.
Airports : George Town (served by commercial airlines), Hog Cay, Rudder Cut Cay, Staniel Cay and Norman's Cay.
Port of Entry : George Town.
Special attractions :
Exuma Land and Sea Park : 22 mile preserve for land and sea life, south of Norman's Cay, between Wax Cay and Conch Cut.
Norman's Cay : Northern island circled by 10 miles of white beaches.
Staniel Cay : About one third of the way from the northern tip of the Exumas. Approach by charter or private plane. Limestone cavern.
Stocking Island : Across the harbour from George Town. Rich in sea shells.
Caves : At Compass Cay (where Thunderball was filmed) and Cave Cay.
George Town : 3 day Out Island Regatta in April.
Harvey Cay : August Monday picnic.

Places to see :
Steventon : Flamingo Fin and Feather Club.
Rolleville : Kermit's Hilltop Restaurant and Tavern.
Little Exuma : Pretty Molly Bay Club.
George Town : Out Island Inn, Pieces of Eight, Club Peace and Plenty.
Docks and Fuel Facilities: Highborne Cay, George Town, Norman's Cay, Compass Cay, Staniel Cay, Sampson Cay.
Boats for Charter: Staniel Cay Yacht Club, Club Peace and Plenty, Out Island Inn.
Skin diving facilities: Out Island Inn, Club Peace and Plenty (snorkeling only) Staniel Cay Yacht Club.
Air Transportation: Daily service between George Town and Nassau, Miami and Fort Lauderdale.
General Store : John Marshall's, George Town.

Long Island.
Population : 4000.
Size : 230 square miles. 60 miles long by 1-5 miles wide.
Airports: Stella Maris (North); Deadman's Cay (Central).
Where to Stay : Stella Maris Inn. Free transportation to and from airport to marina and beaches. Dress casual at all times.
Places of Interest: Within 10 miles of Stella Maris Cape Santa Maria Club and Resort (winter); Columbus Point (two beautiful beaches), Deale's Beach; Simms; Alligator Beach.
Other Places of Interest : Salt Pond; Guana Cay Beach (for shells); Old Bight, site of oldest Spanish church in the Bahamas; Grey's plantation ruins, good beach for coral; Deadman's Cay, large caves; Turtle Cove; Clarence Town; Diamond Crystal Salt Company; Roses; Southernmost Point.

Cat Island.
Size : 48 miles long by 1 to 4 miles wide.
Population : Approximately 3000.
Airstrips: Arthur's Town, The Bight, Hawks Nest Creek, Frankfort Point (Cutlass Bay).
Port of Entry : Arthur's Town, The Bight.
Resorts: Cutlass Bay Club, Hawks Nest Creek Fishing and Yacht Club, Fernandez Bay Club, Pigeon Cay Beach Club.

Places of Interest: Columbus Point (Indian caves); Port Howe (De Veaux Mansion); the Bight (thatched roof houses, plantation ruins, Catholic church); the Hermitage on Mount Alvernia; Old Bight (three miles of unspoilt beach): Fernandez Bay (beaches, high rocks and creeks); Bennett's Harbour village; Little San Salvador (12 miles west of Alligator Point); Goat Cay (north of Little San Salvador).

San Salvador.
Size: 12 miles by 6.
Features: Mt Kerr 140 feet, Great Lake about 10 miles by 2 miles (greatest width).
Where to Stay: Riding Rock Inn; Polaris by the Sea; Jacob Jones Guest House.
Special Interest : Wreck of HMS Conqueror, Britain's first screwbase); Cockburn Town; Sandy Point (ruins of Watling's Castle); Long Bay Beach (Columbus monument); Museum at Polaris by the sea; Graham Harbour.

Rum Cay.
Size: 12 miles by 4–7 miles wide.
Location: 20 miles east of Cape Santa Maria, Long Island and 20 miles southwest of San Salvador.
Settlement: at Port Nelson on south coast, one school.
Where to stay: Rum Cay Club and villas.
Dining: Kay's Bar for seafood.
What to Do: sea sports, duck hunting in winter, fishing.
Special Interest: Wreck of HMS Conqueror, Britain's first screwdriven battleship built in 1855. Off Signal Hill.

K

9 Crooked Island District, Mayaguana, Great Inagua

When Columbus was approaching the Cape which he called Cape Beautiful on the island that the people of San Salvador knew as Saomete but which he 'baptized' Isabella, he smelt a perfume of trees and flowers the 'most delightful in the world'. He took away with him specimens of some of the fruit bearing trees which he did not know but which he was sure were 'very valuable'. He was right at least about one of them because cascarilla bark from Crooked, Long Cay and Acklins islands is still exported today for use in medicines and as an ingredient for a liqueur.

Columbus was captivated by Isabella's songbirds whose voices were so sweet that 'no man would ever want to leave' the island. Isabella was also a nursery of parrots who were so plentiful that their wings obscured the sky when they flew in flocks. There were many other kinds of birds large and small and all very different from the birds he knew in Spain. On Crooked Island, which he had called Isabella after the Spanish Queen, Columbus took in supplies of water and loaded up all the aloes he could find.

The Crooked Island District, which lies eastward of the Crooked Island Passage that divides the archipelago from Long Island, extends from Bird Rock lighthouse in the north for 45 miles to Castle Island lighthouse in the south. The creeks and tidal flats of the islands attract large numbers of tarpon and bonefish. High cliffs and rolling hills ashore recreate for the visitor impressions of that verdant Andalusian spring which Columbus had discovered in late October. The islanders are proud of their reputation as farmers and keep their settlements tidy and well supplied with small parks and recreational grounds. The Blue Hills which are west of the airstrip are clearly visible from the sea. Pitts Town in the extreme northwestern part of the island still has ruins of the first post office to be erected in the Bahamas. Nearby Portland Harbour was visited by Columbus. There is a long white beach between Pitts Town and Landrail Point which has a grove of tall casuarina trees. The town was 'laid out' towards the end of the eighteenth century to meet the needs of the cotton industry. There were once as many as 40 cotton plantations on Crooked Island. G. J. H. Northcroft, author of *Sketches of Summerland*, wrote of visitors in the early 1800s being driven in carriages over good roads amongst smiling cotton fields. Michael Scott, author of *Tom Cringle's Log* (1825), depicts an island dependent upon salt making, turtle catching and dressing some scrubby cotton trees. He immortalized in his pages the postmaster who was a 'stout conch with a square cut coatee and red cape and cuffs'. The postmaster also did a trade with turtle, selling them to passing ships from 'crawls filled with beautiful clean water'. But despite his office and activities as turtle trader Cringle thought he must have had a dull time of it on Crooked Island as there were no other white inhabitants besides 'himself', his wife having gone to Nassau, which he looked upon as the 'prime city of the world' to be confined. By 1906 Crooked Islanders regarded sponging and 'keeping fields' as their major occupations. Crooked Island was undoubtedly a 'most desolate domicile for a lady' in the early nineteenth century, but its neighbour Long Cay (Fortune Island) was to enjoy quite another reputation before the century came to a close. Writing in 1888, L. D. Powles, author of *The Land of the Pink Pearl*, described Long Cay as 'most flourishing' and a 'different world from the rest of the Bahamas'. There, according to Powles, 'men and women, boys and girls, dogs and cats, stores and houses and everything else have an air of freshness and "go" about them, suggestive of life and movement. In all the other out islands things – animate and inanimate alike – remind me of the palace of the sleeping beauty, before the prince's kiss recalled its inmates to conscious existence'.

One of the attractions of Long Cay in the late 'eighties was the circulation of American newspapers 'not more than 4 days old'. These newspapers were brought in by steamers trading between New York, Haiti, Cuba, the West Indies and the Spanish Main. The steamers called at Albert Town to recruit men to join the ships for the round trip. Albert Town was also a collecting port for Bahamians who wanted to work in Jamaica. In much earlier days, Crooked Island had been a valuable outpost of Empire.

Cannons at Marine Farm recall fortifications which together with those at Gun Bluff made Crooked Island Passage safe from attacks by sea. Landrail Point, which today is planted with citrus and other fruit-bearing trees, suffered much from hurricanes and tidal waves, in 1932. A small restaurant and store is appreciated by visitors who are made to feel very welcome by the community. The Commissioner for the Crooked Island District lives at Colonel Hill not far from the 3500 foot Government airstrip. There is a store, restaurant, and guest house at the top of the hill which overlooks the island. The Crooked Island east coast road ends at Cove Landing which is used as an anchorage by local fishermen.

The cays which separate the southern tip of Long Cay at Windsor Point from the southernmost part of Acklins Island were favourite fishing grounds of Franklin D. Roosevelt. Coves and bays of Acklins Island merit titles like Delectable and Lovely. Yachtsmen are particularly welcomed at Chesters, near Lovely Bay in the north of Acklins, where good food, guest rooms, a small supermarket and diesel fuel and gasoline are obtainable. There is an airstrip at Pinefield close to Hilltop View Guest House which has three rooms mostly used by private flyers. There is another airstrip near Spring Point in Delectable Bay. The Deputy Commissioner for Acklins has a residence at Spring Point. A road runs between Lovely Bay in the north and Morant Bay in the centre. There are clinics at Spring Point and Chesters.

Samana or Atwood Cay lies 20 miles north-north-east of the northeastern point of Acklins Island. It is about nine miles long and rises to a height of 100 feet. A freighter is wrecked off the western end of a coral reef which surrounds the island. Almost halfway between the northeast point of Acklins and Mayaguana island are two islands known as the Plana or French Cays. Farmers from Acklins cultivate lands on the French Cays which extend for nine miles and have good beaches on the southern shores.

The Spanish title Mira Por Vos is still the official title of some 40 square miles of reefs, banks and small cays which begin about seven miles west of the Castle Island lighthouse. Another dangerous reef known as Hogsty Reef or Los Corrales lies 37 miles south east of Castle Island about halfway to Great Inagua. Fishermen go to the reef in search of turtles and other marine animals. Most vessels give it a wide berth because throughout the centuries it has proved a graveyard for passing ships. There is a light on north-west Cay which is only about eight feet above the high water mark.

Mayaguana. Mayaguana, an island 24 miles long by six miles at its greatest width, had a population of less than 600 in 1970. Two years later plans were announced for the construction of an 18-mile highway to connect the three main settlements at Abraham's Bay, Pirate's Well and Betsy Bay.

The United States formerly maintained a missile tracking station near Abraham's Bay and the airstrip built for the station is still maintained as the island's airport. There is a commissioner at Abraham's Bay. Fishing around Mayaguana is good and visiting ducks are shot in the winter months. Some crops are raised by the islanders. The island is still thickly covered with lignum vitae, other woods and thick scrub. There are sea gardens offshore between Troublesome and Low Point Hills in Start Bay. Local fishing boats tend to congregate at the north eastern tip of the island inside the reef to the south of Booby Cay. In 1960 Abraham's Bay was devastated by a hurricane.

Great Inagua. Except for James Hill and Salt Pond Hill, which are both 90 feet above sea level, and East Hill which rises to a height of 132 feet, Inagua is low and flat over its 40 miles of length and 20 miles of average width. The island has a flamingo population of about 30,000 resident birds who live in a sanctuary in the interior managed jointly by the Audubon Society and the Bahamas National Trust. The flamingos of Inagua are the remnants of a group of birds who once flourished as far north as the polar regions and whose numbers have been steadily decreasing in recent years. The greatest protection they have in Inagua is the wildness of the island, which has been described as the most desolate of all in the archipelago of the Bahamas. At the turn of this century G. J. H. Northcroft described Inagua as 'the

Beersheba of the Bahamas, on the threshold of the West Indies'.

Inagua has a great shallow lake about 12 miles long. The waters of Lake Windsor are feeding grounds for flamingos, spoonbills, ducks and other birds. They also help to propagate the giant mosquitoes which have been vividly described as 'leeches on wings'. A pilot who passed through Inagua to refuel in the 'sixties told me that the mosquitoes were the first signs of life he found at the deserted airstrip. They were so much in possession of the island, he said, that 'they don't move when you bring your hand down to crush them'.

Inagua lies north of the Windward passage which separates the eastern tip of Cuba from the northwestern tip of Haiti. It is 325 nautical miles from Nassau and belongs geographically with the Turks and Caicos Islands which also have dry climates and are swept by the trade winds.

It has been well said that the sound of the surf provides a tone background for life on Inagua, where everything ashore owes its existence to the outpouring of the ocean beds. It is an island of shimmering heat waves, glistening white beaches, headlands bristling with razor-sharp stone needles, and brilliant blue ocean bursting into waves of white spumes gushing upwards across moss-covered rocks. The wild inhospitable land is softened by moonlight and at Man of War Bay long rows of coconut trees face towards a blue calm sea. The smallest lizard in the world, the Sphaerodactylus, breeds on Inagua. Other animal denizens are thousands of hermit crabs, hundreds of wild donkeys, land crabs, bats (in caves), doves, mocking birds and humming birds.

The colour, which is so inconspicuous ashore except on flowering trees, roseate spoonbills and prim flamingos, is everywhere present under the sea off Inagua. Only a few miles from Mathew Town on the outer edge of the Great Reef are forests of yellow coral trees growing around dark caverns and bright blue patches of ocean. In between their upswept leafless branches swim fish bedecked in vermilion, purple, lavender, mauve, pink, yellow, silver and emerald green. On the rocks sea worms display their flower-like fintails among sponges of red, green and lavender.

A paradise for naturalists ashore or undersea, Inagua has relied mostly on the production of salt to feed its human family. A revival of the salt industry was started by the Erickson Brothers who formed West Indian Chemicals Ltd. in 1935. By 1941 the value of exports had reached £34,489. In the 1950s the Morton Salt Company took over salt production on Inagua and by 1971 had brought output to over one million tons of salt. The Morton Salt Company like the Diamond Crystal Salt Company on Long Island extracts its salt by solar plant. The growth of the salt industry in recent years has given Mathew Town electricity, a hospital and cinema. At last count there were three schools on Inagua catering for 419 pupils. The resident population at the time of the 1970 census was 1109 divided nearly equally between males and females.

Mathew Town is a port of entry to the Bahamas, but there are no natural harbours on Great Inagua which is for the most part surrounded by reefs. In good weather visiting yachtsmen may anchor under the northern shore of Man of War Bay, but local pilots are required to find safe anchorages when winds are unfavourable. Ocean Bight on the north of the island is unfriendly because of its line of steep stone cliffs. Mathew Town has grocery and hardware stores, ice and telecommunications. The roads are good and there is an airstrip near the town. The salt company runs a guest house and there are some small inns and lodging houses.

Little Inagua, a low island of about 30 square miles five miles north of the northeastern part of Great Inagua, is inhabited by birds, wild donkeys and goats. People go there sometimes to fish.

SUMMARY :

Crooked Island District.
Population : Crooked Island 700 : Acklins 1000.
Location :
North to South : 45 miles from Bird Rock lighthouse on Crooked island to Castle island lighthouse, south of Acklins Island.
West to East : 30 miles from Bird Rock to Hell Gate at north end of Acklins Island.
What to See : Rolling hills, neat villages, farms, scenic creeks, harbours, ancient fortifications.
Special Interest : Landrail Point and Colonel Hill on Crooked

Island, Chesters, Lovely Bay, Hilltop View Guest House, Hard Hill on Acklins Island.

Mayaguana.
Location : 50 miles east of Acklins Island.
Size : 24 miles long by 6 miles (at widest point).
Population : Approximately 6000.
Special interest : Woods, sea gardens, fishing.
Largest settlement : Abraham's Bay, Commissioner's residence, airstrip.

Great Inagua.
Location : 325 miles south east of Nassau to the south of Windward Passage separating Cuba from Haiti.
Size : Approximately 40 miles long by 20 miles wide.
Population : Over 1100.
Special features : 12 mile lake preserved as flamingo sanctuary; East Hill 132 feet.
Port of Entry : Mathew Town, headquarters of Morton Salt Company.
Airstrip : Near Mathew Town.
Fair weather anchorage : Man of War Bay.

10 The Bahamas: General Information

Climate: The islands south of the Tropic of Cancer have less seasonal variation than the majority which lie to the north. Grand Bahama and the Abacos have cooler winters than New Providence where mean temperatures range from 69° 6' F in January to 70° 9' in December with temperatures in excess of 80° F between June and September.

Mean relative humidity is between 77 and 82 per cent for all months of the year.

Although cloudy weather can occur at any time of the year average daily sunshine hours exceed seven.

Nassau receives about twice as much rainfall as the southern tropical islands of the archipelago and about one quarter less than the more northerly islands. Mean rainfall for Nassau is 52.8 inches per year with more than eight inches in June and October and more than six from July to September.

Time: Normally 5 hours behind Greenwich Mean Time or the same as Eastern Standard Time.

In some summer months Eastern Daylight Time, 4 hours behind GMT is employed.

Clothing: Informal and light. Cotton skirts, blouses, dresses and shorts for women. Sport shirts and shorts or slacks for men. Changes of swimsuits and shorts. For dinner light jacket with tie or cravat for men with long lightweight trousers. In winter ladies need light sweaters or scarves.

In large hotels guests are expected to wear beach jackets or wraps between room and outdoor pools or beach areas.

Beach clothes or very brief shorts are not regarded as suitable wear in towns.

High Season : mid December to late April.

Drinking Water : Varies. New Providence and Grand Bahama have adequate supplies of pure water filtered and chlorinated. Marsh Harbour has chlorinated piped water. All resort areas have potable water. Water is distilled, or taken from surface wells or rainwater is normally available at stores and supermarkets.

Electricity : supply is normally 120 volts 60 cycles. Unless electric razors are geared to several voltages an adaptor should be packed.

Hospital and Medical Service : Private practitioners in Nassau and Freeport. Over 40 clinics in Out islands, some with resident doctors and dentists. Nassau has the government operated Princess Margaret Hospital (425 beds) and the privately operated Rassin hospital (26 beds). In Freeport government operates the Rand Memorial Hospital (75 beds) and there are two privately operated institutions, the Antonio Clinic and the Lucayan Medical Group.

A flying doctor service is operated by the Princess Margaret Hospital for special patients in Out islands.

Special Taxes and Tolls : Airline and steamship tickets issued in the Bahamas are subject to a $2 tax.

Hotel taxes of 4 per cent European rate are added to bills in Nassau and Freeport. In other islands a flat rate of 50 cents per night is added for each guest.

A toll of $2 is charged for each motor vehicle crossing the bridge to Paradise Island. Pedestrians or non-motorized vehicles have to pay 25 cents toll.

Departure taxes are not charged for children under three years old; a charge of $1.50 is levied on each child aged between 3 and 12 years and $3 on each adult. These taxes are levied at airports and seaports.

Money : Bahamian currency consists of notes in denominations of $100, $50, $20, $10, $5, $3, $1 and fifty cents; and coins in denominations of $5, $2, $1, fifty cents, 25 cents, 15 cents, 10 cents, five cents and one cent.

On 12 February 1973 parity with the US dollar was proclaimed. US and Bahamian dollars are interchangeable in the islands.

Travellers' cheques in sterling or dollars are accepted by most large hotels and stores. Personal cheques are unlikely to be accepted and only some credit cards.

Banking Hours: Banks are closed on Saturdays.

Hours of opening vary on the Out-islands.

Commercial banks in New Providence open between 9.30 am and 3.30 pm Monday to Thursday and from 9.30 am to 5 pm on Friday.

In Freeport, Grand Bahama banks open at 9 am and close at 1 pm Monday to Thursday. On Friday they open and close at the same time but reopen between 4 pm and 6 pm. Foreign exchange booths are open daily between 9.30 am and 5.30 pm in the arrival zone of Nassau's airport and between 9 am and 5.30 pm in the departure zone.

Tipping: Fifteen per cent customary except in hotels and restaurants with fixed service charges. Normal tips in bars is 10 per cent. These rates are compulsory in Nassau and Paradise Island.

Immigration and Customs: Must be cleared at the first point of entry into the Bahamas and at the last point of departure.

Duplicate immigration card stamped by the Immigration officer on arrival must be surrendered on departure.

Although passports are not required of certain visitors including British Commonwealth citizens on visits of less than three weeks, they are required for re-entry to many countries. British Commonwealth citizens, US citizens and the citizens of many other specific countries do not require visas. Luggage is subject to customs inspection. Firearms may not be taken into the Bahamas without a gun licence issued by the local government. Possession of narcotic drugs is a criminal offence.

An adult is permitted to bring in personal effects free of duty. In addition every adult is allowed duty free the choice of 50 cigars, 200 cigarettes or one pound of tobacco and a quart bottle of alcoholic liquor. Special permits are required to import animals.

Health Regulations: Visitors should always clear with their home authorities what certificates are currently required for re-entry. Smallpox vaccination certificate is no longer required for entry to the Bahamas or for re-entry to Britain from the islands. Health requirements in the Bahamas are minimal.

Private Plane Flying: A brochure of this title is issued by the Ministry of Tourism. It gives details of airports, landing and navigational facilities, communication, fuel and repair stations and other data.

Land: About 110 of the estimated 5,400 square miles of land in the Bahamas is privately owned.

Public Holidays: (subject to change). New Year's Day, Good Friday, Easter Monday, May 25 (Queen Victoria's birthday), June 1 (Labour Day), June 11 (Whit Monday), July 10 (Independence Day), August 6 (Emancipation Day), October 12 (Discovery Day), Christmas Day, December 26 (Boxing Day).

Stores: On New Providence and most islands stores are closed on public holidays. Some stores close at noon on Friday and are open all Saturday. Others may remain open on Friday afternoon but are closed on Saturday afternoon. Normal opening hours are from 9 am to 5 pm.

What to Buy:
IMPORTED: a wide range including perfumes, liquors, watches, jewellery, cameras, pipes, men's and women's clothes; knitting supplies.
LOCAL: Bahamian tortoiseshell articles, Bahamian handprints Androsia tropical fabrics, ceramic chickcharnies, loop earrings, shellwork, straw goods, paintings, records.

PRICES: are fixed in stores, variable in stalls and 'Market places'.

Services: Many Bahamian stores will despatch purchases other than liquor to any overseas address. Liquor stores deliver to hotel or ship.

Traffic: Follows the left side of the road. In Nassau look out for motorcycles, bicycles, carriages and pedestrians.

Post: Letters airmail to US and Canada 15 cents per half ounce. To United Kingdom, Europe, Central and South America, Bermuda, West Indies, 18 cents per half ounce.
　　Postcards Airmail to all destinations 11 cents.

Laundry: Arrangements through hotel desk.

Spectator Sports: Soccer, baseball, volley ball, squash and softball.
　　Horse racing Tuesday and Saturday afternoon from January 2 to April 15.
Active Sports: Tennis, swimming, diving, golf, horseback riding, polo, water skiing, fishing, motor boating, sailing, para-sailing, snorkel and scuba.

Underwater: All inshore waters on northern side of New Providence Island are a nature reserve in which it is not permitted to kill or remove fish or any other marine products while using *any* underwater equipment.
　　Outside the reserved areas it is permissible to use snorkels, Hawaiian slings or hand spears for underwater fishing or collecting marine products. It is forbidden to employ scuba or breathing apparatus, guns or missiles for such purposes.

Fishing:
YEAR ROUND: Tarpon (Andros and Bimini); Barracuda (everywhere); Bonefish (throughout islands); Grouper (around reefs throughout); Allison and Yellow Tuna (Deep water areas, most plentiful in June to August); Blue Marlin (Best months June and July).

SUMMER AND AUTUMN: Sailfish (Berry Islands, Chub Cay, Bimini, Cat Cay, West End, Walkers' Cay, Exuma Sound).

MAY 7 TO JUNE 15: Giant (Bluefin) Tuna (Bimini, Cat Cay, West End).

MAY TO SEPTEMBER: Blackfin Tuna and Oceanic Bonito. Deep water areas.

WINTER AND SPRING: Dolphin. Deep water areas. White Marlin from Bimini to Eleuthera; from Walker's Cay to Exuma Sound.

NOVEMBER TO APRIL: Wahoo. Deep water areas. Best months January and February.

NOVEMBER TO MAY: Amberjack. Around reefs and creeks throughout.

The Bahamians have 43 world records registered with the International Game Fish Association.

Hunting: Visitors need to rent guns for shooting in open seasons.

15 September to 28 February: Open season for marsh hens, white crowned pigeons, wood doves, quail doves, ringnecked pheasants, Florida gallinules, guinea fowls, black or yellow crowned herons.

15 September to 31 March: Open season for Florida doves, wild ducks, geese (Not whistling ducks), bobwhite quail, chuckar partridge, jack snipe, coot.

No open season for other birds.

The Ministry of Agriculture and Fisheries has a list of places where killing or catching birds is illegal at all times.

Wildlife Reserves: Exuma Cays, Land and Sea Park, Inagua Flamingo Park, Pelican Cays, Peterson Cay and many bird sanctuaries and underwater protected areas.

Telephone: Most islands are linked through the Telecommunication Corporation in Nassau by radio channels. Collect or credit card payments are usually accepted. Hotel desks should be consulted in the out islands. *Out island telephone service is normally daytime service.*

New Providence and Freeport have direct dial service between the islands and with the United States. They also have 24-hour telephone and telegraph service to many overseas countries. Radio teleprinter service is available at Nassau and Freeport. The Bahamas are linked to the Cable and Wireless world cable chain via Bermuda, and a submarine cable to West Palm Beach.

Local Transport:
On Land: Taxis, rental cars, motor scooters, bicycles, small buses (irregular), charter buses, Surreys (Nassau).
On sea: Powerboats, sailboats, mailboats (irregular).
By air: Bahamas Airways, charter planes, private planes.

Water Skiing and Motor Boat Control: Except for purposes of approach or departure water skiing or motorboating is prohibited within 200 feet of the shore line. A second person to act as lookout is required in motorboat during water skiing. Persons under 16 may not drive a motorboat unless supervised by someone aged 16 or over.

Bahamas Air Sea Rescue Association: Has 40 boats and 10 aircraft, keeps 24 hour watch with over 100 volunteer members through the islands. Works in co-operation with United States Coast Guards.

Radio: Radio Station ZNS I operates 24 hours daily on 1540 kilocycles. Weather reports are broadcast by this station at frequent intervals and on ZNS II (1240), and by stations on the US mainland.

Full radio facilities for yachtsmen are published in the *Yachtsman's Guide to the Bahamas*, an official publication of the Ministry of Tourism.

Nassau and Miami operate a marine radio service, UNICOM (122.8) is used throughout the islands between aircraft, resorts, taxis, and individual subscribers.

Charts: 69 detailed cruising charts of the Bahamas Islands are published by Tropic Isle Publishers Inc., P.O. Box 866, Coral Gables, Florida 33134, publishers of the *Yachtsman's Guide*.

Control Zone Airports:
Grand Bahama: Jack Tar International, Freeport International.
Eleuthera: Rock Sound.

New Providence : Nassau International.

Airstrips open to visitors : Walkers Cay, Treasure Cay, Marsh Harbour, Sandy Point, Acklins, San Andros, Andros Town, Congo Town, Great Harbour Cay, Chub Cay, South Bimini, Arthur's Town, New Bight, Cutlass Bay, Hawksnest, Crooked Island, North Eleuthera, Norman's Cay, Staniel Cay, George Town, Inagua, Cape Santa Maria, Stella Maris, Deadman's Cay, Hard Bargain, South Point, San Salvador, Rum Cay, South Caicos, Providenciales International, Grand Turk.

Specimen Cruises from Nassau :
  Nassau Bar to Fresh Creek Andros and return : 68 miles 2 days minimum.
  Nassau Bar to Little Harbour Cay and return : 66 miles 3-4 days minimum.
  Nassau Bar to Harbour Island and return (via Current Island 31 miles from Nassau Bar) : 87 miles 3-4 days minimum.
  Nassau to Rock Sound via Hatchet Bay and Governor's Harbour (Return by way of Allan's Cay) : 180 miles 5-6 days minimum.
  Nassau to Allan's Cay and return : 68 miles 2 days minimum.
  Nassau to Farmer's Cay and return; 186 miles 3-4 days minimum.
  Nassau to George Town and return : 266 miles 4 days and over.
  Nassau Bar to Little Harbour, Abaco and return : 155 miles.
  Nassau Bar to Man of War, Abaco and return : 190 miles.
  Nassau Bar to Green Turtle Cay, Abaco and return : 236 miles.
  Nassau Bar to Walkers Cay and return : 386 miles.
  At least 2 weeks are needed to explore the Abaco Cays.

Cruising Facilities :
  Bimini : Big Game Fishing Club, Brown's Dock, Blue Water Marina, Weeche's Dock.
  South Bimini : Bimini Islands Yacht Club, Buccaneer Point Marina.
  Cat Cay : Cat Cay Dock.
  Berry Islands : Tamboo Marina, Crown Colony Club.
  New Providence : Coral Harbour, Lyford Cay (private) Club, Nassau Harbour Club, Bayshore Marina, Nassau Yacht Club,

Brown's Boat Basin, Paradise Island Marina, East Bay Yacht Basin.

Grand Bahama: Grand Bahama Marina, West End, Harbour Inn Marina, Running Mon Marina, Deep Water Cay Club.

The Abacos: Walker Cay Club, Crown Haven Marina, Cooper's Town, Bluff House Marina, Green Turtle Club, Other Shore Club, Town Dock, Treasure Cay, Guana Harbour Club, Man of War Cay, Hope Town Lighthouse Marina, White Sound Fin and Tail Inn, Marsh Harbour, Gold Port Marina.

Andros: Andros Beach Hotel, Andros Yacht Club, Mangrove Cay.

The Eleutheras: Sawyer's Marina, Town Dock, Echo Marina, Harbour Island Town Dock, Briland Yacht Club, Current Club, Hatchet Bay, Eleuthera Marina, Davis Harbour, Cape Eleuthera.

The Exumas: Highborne Cay, Norman's Cay, Sampson's Cay, Staniel Bay Yacht Club, Kenneth's Dock, Exuma Services George Town.

Long Island: Stella Maris Marina, Blue Haven Ltd Salt Pond, Clarence Town Dock.

Cat Island: Hawk's Nest Yacht Club.

Seaports of Entry:

The Abacos: Green Turtle Cay/Treasure Cay, Grand Cay, Marsh Harbour, Sandy Point.

Andros: Nicoll's Town, San Andros, Fresh Creek, Mangrove Cay, Congo Town.

Berry Islands: Great Harbour Cay, Chub Cay.

Bimini: Alice Town North Bimini.

Cat Cay: Cat Cay Club.

Eleuthera: Harbour Island, Hatchet Bay, Governor's Harbour, Rock Sound.

Exuma: George Town.

Grand Bahama: West End, Freeport, Lucaya.

Inagua: Mathew Town.

Mayaguana: Abraham's Bay.

New Providence: Nassau.

Ragged Island: Duncan Town.

San Salvador: Cockburn Town.

Treasure: About $360 million of treasure and coins is estimated

M

to be still sunk in Bahamian waters. In 1964 the Lucayan treasure of silver coins worth about $7½ million was discovered about 1000 yards from Freeport in ten feet of water.

Special Dishes: Raw Conch with salads. Chowder and turtle soups. Green turtle baked in shell. Broiled crawfish. Baked Nassau grouper. Nassau Peas'n Rice. Red Snapper fillets in anchovy sauce. Baked crab.

Bahamian Sweets: Rum raisin ice cream. Coconut and rum custard pudding.

How to Get to Bahamas by air:
British Airways from London via Bermuda, or Miami, or New York.
International Air Bahamas from Luxembourg.
Lufthansa from Frankfurt, Cologne, Merida (Yucatan).
Sabena from Brussels and Mexico City.
Quantas from Sidney via Fiji, Tahiti, Acapulco and Mexico City; from London.
Air Canada from Toronto, Montreal and Jamaica.
Air Jamaica from Chicago, Boston, Baltimore, Washington, Detroit, Jamaica.
Delta from Boston, New York.
Pan American from New York, Miami, Fort Lauderdale.
Eastern from Miami, Fort Lauderdale, Pittsburgh, Philadelphia, St Louis, Tampa, Atlanta, Baltimore.
Northeast from New York.
Shawnee from Fort Lauderdale, West Palm Beach.
Mackey International from Florida.
Bahamasair from Florida.

How to Get to Bahamas by sea:
Cruises by P and O Lines from the United Kingdom.
Cruises from New York and Florida; Home Lines, Eastern Steamship, Norwegian Caribbean, Norwegian American, Atlantic Cruise, Costa.
Passenger services from Antwerp and Amsterdam.

Tourist Offices:
  United Kingdom : 23, Old Bond Street, London.
  West Germany : 6000 Frankfurt/Main, Zimmerweg 10.
  Canada : 85 Richmond Street West, Toronto 110, Ontario.

Driving Licence: Anyone over 17 with a valid driving licence of their country of residence can drive for 3 months without a Bahamian licence. Speed limits average between 15 and 45 miles per hour.

Cinemas and Theatres: Airconditioned and 'drive in' in Nassau and Freeport. Civic Theatre in Nassau. Son-et-Lumière nightly at Fort Charlotte, Nassau.

Education: Students enrolled in government schools for the year 1970-71 were 39,630 of whom 22,313 or 57 per cent were living on New Providence. Another 13,107 students were enrolled in independent schools of whom 10,177 lived in New Providence. There are teacher training colleges and institutions for technical and vocational training. Scholarships are offered to overseas universities. The Bahamas contribute to the University of the West Indies which conducts extra mural activity in the islands. The Ministry of Education and Culture is responsible for the Archives, the Bahamas Library Service and Sports and recreation in schools.
  Education is compulsory and free for children between 5 and 14. There were 212 primary and secondary schools in the Bahamas in 1973. About 90 per cent of the population is literate.

Taxation: Duties between 20 and 40 per cent of landed cost provide most of the revenue. There is a modest property tax but no direct income taxes, death duties or inheritance taxes.

Development: The Bahamas Development Corporation established in 1973 is made up of private business men and government officials. The Corporation's policy is to maintain control of government property and to develop it or lease it for industrial or business use in well chosen areas. It aims to keep residential areas free of commercial traffic. It assists local and foreign investors through liaison with government agencies. Through its operation the government becomes a partner with private developers of residential, resort, recreational, industrial and commercial projects.

Incentives: Manufacturers operating in the Bahamas have complete exemption for 15 years on all earnings. There is no corporate tax, no personal tax, no capital gains tax, no profits tax, no real estate tax, no inheritance tax. Complete freedom is given to repatriate profits. Industrial estates are provided on New Providence and Grand Bahama.

No customs duties are levied on machines, tools, raw materials or components necessary for plant operation.

Cargo Services: The Bahamas have direct air cargo services with the United States, Canada, Europe, South America, other Caribbean countries, Mexico, Australia and Japan. Seventeen shipping lines provide over 60 scheduled cargo sailings monthly.

Finance: More than 100 international banks and finance have registered offices in the Bahamas. Among the major clearing banks are First National City Bank, Chase Manhattan Bank, Bank of London and Montreal, Royal Bank of Canada, and Barclays.

Power: Government and privately owned plants provide electric power. Water, gas and fuel oil are available for business use in major islands. In 1971 electricity produced was 320 million kilowatt hours.

Labour: Maximum use is made of Bahamians. Basic training is available at the Technical Institute on New Providence. Foreign technical, managerial and supervisory personnel are admitted when Bahamians are not available to fill vacancies.

The work force has been estimated at about 68,000. About 20 per cent of the population is considered to be of Haitian origin. In 1971 there were 18 registered trade unions and 15 Employers' Associations.

Chamber of Commerce: Maintains active standing committees which are concerned with major aspects of economic development. It is a member of the Chamber of Commerce of the Americas, the Federation of Commonwealth Chambers of Commerce and a member of the Caribbean Association of Industry and Commerce.

Cost of Living: In 1973 the Chamber of Commerce estimated that a family of three would need between $12,000 and $15,000 a year to enjoy a reasonable standard.

Government: The Bahamas became independent on 10 July 1973. The Governor General is representative of the Queen in the Bahamas. There is a Senate of 16 members, 9 appointed by the majority party, 4 by the opposition and three by the Governor General. The House of Assembly has 38 members, of whom 21 are elected by people in 'family island' constituencies and 17 by voters on New Providence.

Under the Constitution of 1969 the Bahamas were officially designated as the Commonwealth of the Bahama Islands.

Population: Of a total population of 168,812 in 1970, over 100,000 or 60.1 per cent lived on New Providence and over 25,000 or 15.3 per cent lived on Grand Bahama. Nearly 10,000 or 5.6 per cent lived on Eleuthera, Harbour Island, Spanish Wells and neighbouring islands. Andros the largest island of the Bahamas has no more than 5.2 per cent of the population.

Trade: Between 1960 and 1970 the Bahamas exported 73.4 per cent of its products to the United States. These were mostly crawfish, cucumbers, crude salt, pulpwood, tomatoes, cement, eggplant, sugar, residual fuel oils, bunker and rum. Total value of goods exported to the United States during the period was £234.5 million. Between 1960 and 1970 the Bahamas imported most of its goods from the United States. Foodstuffs, beverages and tobacco over the period were valued at $238.9 million and accounted for 23.5 per cent of all goods imported from the United States.

In 1970 Libya and Liberia supplied 40 per cent of the crude petroleum imported into the Bahamas.

The Bahamas had an adverse visible trade balance of $229 million in 1970 and a favourable invisible balance of $120 million. Tourist receipts in 1970 were $221 million.

Bahamasair : The national flag carrier connects the major islands of the Bahamas and the Turks and Caicos Islands and operates BAC 1-11 jets between Nassau, Freeport and Miami with authority to provide additional services to Fort Lauderdale, West Palm Beach and Tampa. It is 51 per cent government owned.

During the year ended in June 1974 Bahamasair earned about $9 million and carried 480,000 passengers. The company was formed on 18 June 1973 through amalgamation of Flamingo Airlines and Out Island Airways. In that year it employed 410 people and had an annual payroll of $2.8 million.

Goombay Summer : A 3 month festival to give the visitor 'real value for money spent'. Provided by the Ministry of Tourism it is supported by the Nassau/Paradise Island Promotion Board, the Freeport/Lucaya Tourist and Convention Board and the Bahamas Hotel Association. First Goombay was in 1971. Goombay or Bahamian Folk music resembles West Indian calypso.

Bahamian Flag : Turquoise, gold and black. First unfurled at noon on 10 July 1973 at Fort Charlotte in the presence of over 50,000 people.

Bahamas National Trust : Maintains close liaison with the World Wild Life Fund, the National Society of America, the Smithsonian Institution, the New York Zoological Society, the American Museum of Natural History and other Conservation bodies. Has established seven national parks and wildlife sanctuaries :—

Exuma Cays Land and Sea Park : 176 square miles.

Inagua Park : 287 square miles of wilderness; Habitat for over 25,000 flamingos.

Union Creek (Inagua) : Green Turtle Breeding Project in co-operation with the Caribbean Conservation Corporation.

Pelican Cays Land and Sea Park: Undersea caves, coral reefs, fish, plant and bird life off Great Abaco.

South-East Abaco: woodland sanctuary of the Bahamian Parrot.

Peterson Cay Park (Grand Bahama): coral gardens with fish, marine animal and plant life.

Conception Island: Sanctuary for migratory and other birds, laying beaches for green turtles.

Water-Catchments are maintained on some Out-islands for migrating birds in transit between North and South America.

Chronology

31 August 1649	Act for the Adventurers for the Eleutherian islands constituted Sayle and associates proprietors of the islands
1650	Eleutherian settlers give Harvard ten tons of braziletto wood
1652–54	First Dutch War
1656	Governor of Jamaica ordered by English government to evacuate settlers from Eleuthera
1665–67	Second Dutch War
1666	'Sayle's island' settled, later known as New Providence
1667	Treaty of Breda. Turning point in Anglo-Dutch relations. Clarendon goes into exile
1670	Treaty with Spain. First recognition by Spain of British Sovereignty in West Indies
	Shaftesbury's Act against spiriting or kidnapping Englishmen to work as forced labourers in colonies
1 Nov 1670	Charles II granted Bahama islands to six Lords Proprietors of Carolina
1671	Morgan sacked Panama
24 April 1671	Proprietors appoint first Governor of Bahamas
1672–74	Shaftesbury heads opposition in England
1680	Anglo-Spanish Treaty called for 'real peace beyond the line' and recognised *right of English to trade in West Indian waters*
1681	Shaftesbury flees to Amsterdam
1682	Spaniards deport planters from South Bahamas to Cuba
1683	Shaftesbury flees to Amsterdam.
1684	Spaniards captured New Providence
	Majority of settlers went as refugees to Jamaica and Massachusetts
1685	Duke of Monmouth's rebellion
1687	Albemarle's discovery of Spanish treasure between Tortuga and Caicos
1688	James II vacates English throne
	Grand Jury of Bermuda petition for annexation of New Providence. Return of settlers from

L

	Jamaica under Thomas Bridges as Governor
1689–97	War with France
1690	Inauguration of Colonel Cadwallader Jones, 'the pirate's governor', in New Providence
1695	Governor Nicholas Trott laid out Charles Town (later renamed Nassau)
1697	Fort Nassau completed
	Treaty of Ryswick. Peace with France
1699	Bahamas Assembly pass anti-piracy act
	Governor Webb escapes to Delaware
	Deputy Governor Read Elding hangs 5 pirates
October 1701	Civil rebellion. Governor expelled. President elected
1702–13	War of the Spanish succession
1703	French-Spanish expedition from Havana sacks Nassau
1706	Spanish report of few survivors on New Providence, scattered in 'little huts, ready upon assault to secure themselves in the woods'
1707	Union of England and Scotland Act
1708	John Graves addresses a Memorial to Proprietors and Commissioners of Customs relating to bad government of Bahamas
1713	Treaty of Utrecht
1714	Bermuda's Governor reports on the state of anarchy in the Bahamas
1717	The Governor of Virginia petitions the English Government to secure the trade of the American coasts and to dislodge the pirates from the Bahamas, where they have settled their 'general rendezvous and seem to look upon these islands as their own'
28 Oct 1717	Lords Proprietors hand over civil and military government of Bahamas to the Crown. Quit rents and royalties leased to Company of London and Bristol merchants and Woodes Rogers for 21 years
6 Feb 1718	King George 1 appoints Woodes Rogers Captain General and Governor in Chief of Bahama Islands

18 July 1718	Woodes Rogers proclaims martial law in Bahamas
	Later in year New Providence ravaged by an epidemic
	Cat Island attacked by Spaniards
	Round-up of pirates in Exumas
10 Dec 1718	Execution of ten pirates
February 1720	Nassau attacked by Spaniards. Landing repulsed
August 1721	Woodes Rogers returns to Bristol. Imprisoned for debts incurred in Bahamas
25 August 1729	Woodes Rogers back as Governor of Bahamas
29 Sep 1729	Inauguration of House of Assembly
1731	Publication in London of Mark Catesby's Natural History of Carolina, Florida and the Bahama Islands
15 July 1732	Woodes Rogers dies in Nassau
1733	Lords Proprietors are paid £1000 each and the Company £2000 for unexpired lease of Bahamas
	Bourbon family compact between France and Spain
1734	First Bahamian revenue bills
1737–41	House of Assembly prorogued
1738	House of Commons in England discuss the purchase of the 'strategic Bahamas'
1740	John Tinker appointed Governor
1742–8	Nassau a 'station for privateering trade'
1748–56	Years of depression
1756–63	Renewal of privateering trade
1762	British fleet captured Havana
1763	Britain returns Havana and Manila to Spain in exchange for Florida, which was to remain British until 1783
1764	French occupy Grand Turk island for brief period
1766	Declaratory Act assented supremacy of British Parliament over American legislatures.
1767	Governor Shirley recommends free port status for Nassau. No success till 20 years later

1770	Governor Thomas Shirley told by British Government to legislate for Turks islanders and to tax them
3 March 1776	American invasion of Nassau for 2 weeks Forts dismantled, Governor and Inspector General taken as hostages
January 1778	American marines invade Nassau for 2 days Many Bahamians join American forces
1779	Turks and Caicos islands represented in Bahamian House of Assembly
1780	Recall of Governor Montfort Browne The Bahamas used as privateering bases
7 May 1782	Governor Maxwell surrendered to Cuban Governor Don Juan de Cargigal Spaniards occupy the Bahamas
1783	French forces seize Turks islands Article of Treaty of Versailles stipulates restoration of the islands of Providence and the Bahamas without exception. Peace treaty signed 3 September 1783
April 1783	Deveaux of South Carolina and his 'ragged militia' recapture New Providence
1783–88	Settlement of Out Islands
Sept 1783	Settlement at Carleton, Abaco
1784	First newspaper, the Bahama Gazette printed in August Marsh Harbour, Abaco settled Provision made for 5 new Out island constituencies to be represented in House of Assembly
1785	Governor Maxwell abandons office and leaves for England English settlers advised to leave Florida for the Bahamas
1787	Nassau becomes free port. Trade with Cuba, Mexico and Spanish Central America. Lords Proprietors surrender titles to Bahamas and receive £2000 each
1788–1796	Earl of Dunmore, Governor Builds forts, public buildings, houses

1789	Total population of the Bahamas estimated at 11,300
	Outbreak of cotton disease: chenille bug
1795–1803	Evacuation of plantations on Long Island
1796	Hurricane. Yellow fever outbreak
	Negro Joseph Paul founded Wesleyan Church
1800	Barbadian Rev William Turton began Methodist mission in Nassau
	St Matthew's church built
1800–15	Period of gracious colonial house-building in Nassau
1805	Beginning of planter emigration caused by soil exhaustion
1807	Abolition of Slave Trade
1813	Hurricane
1822	Slave population on 17 islands 10,808
1830	Columbus's statue erected in Nassau
1833	Slavery abolished
	Baptist Missionary Society founded Zion church
1834	Four coloured members in House of Assembly
1835	Board of Education established for Bahamas. Reform of magistracy
1837	Foundation stone of Cathedral laid
1 Aug 1838	Bahamian slaves fully freed
1840	Regular steamship service between Liverpool and Boston
1841	Separation of Executive and Legislative Councils
1843	Nassau distributing point for Royal Mail Steam Packet Company (Suspended a few years later)
1844	Year of drought. Sisal planting started. Nassau Guardian started
1848	Turks and Caicos islands separated from Bahamas, under jurisdiction of Jamaica
1858–64	313 wrecks reported
1859	Cunard agree to connect New York and Nassau. 26 public schools with only 39 teachers
1860	Construction of Royal Victoria Hotel begins
1861	Anglican See of Nassau formed

	First Confederate vessel arrived at Nassau from Charleston with cotton
	The Bahamas classified by Select Committee of House of Commons as outpost of imperial defence
1862–65	Period of prosperity through blockade running
	Outbreak of yellow fever in 1862
1863–75	Bishop Addington Venables, a disciple of the Oxford Movement
1864	5,949 registered electors
	Bahamian Police Force created
1866	Hurricane
	A tidal wave over Hog Island
	Cable laid across the Atlantic
1868	Large deficits of revenue
	Foundation of Royal Colonial Institute
1869	Bill to amend the ecclesiastical laws of Bahamas
1870–1946	British Empire as World Power
1877	Compulsory education Act for New Providence children aged 6-12
1879	Steamship connection with New York
1885	Public Bank goes into bankruptcy in Nassau
	Foundation of St Francis Xavier's church on West Street
1886	Bahamas and West Indies take part in Colonial and Indian Exhibition, London
1887	Over £100,000 invested in sisal plantations
1891	Telegraph service with Florida
	Withdrawal of Imperial troops
	Police recruited in Barbados
	Population of Bahamas 47,565
1892	Pineapple exports valued at £60,000
	Training school for teachers established
1892–1902	Period of comparative prosperity
	Revenue increased by more than 32 per cent
1893	Dunmore House bought by Father Schreiner for Catholic priory (previously used by West Indian Regiment as Officers' Mess 1842-91)
1895	Cable laid between Nassau and Florida

	Radio adopted for Wireless telegraphy
1897	Compulsory Education for all children aged up to 14
1898	Fourth Hotel and Steamship Act of Bahamas House of Assembly
	H. M. Flager renovated Victoria Hotel
1900	Hotel Colonial opened
1902	Sisal exports valued at £37,574
	Population of Bahamas 55,190
1906	Bahamas Timber Company began operation at Wilson City, Abaco
1907	First telephone system installed in Bahamas
1908	Royal Bank of Canada opens Nassau branch
1909	Electricity in Nassau
1917	Record sponge exports valued at £152,000
1919	New Assembly convened. First since 1910
	First seaplanes visit Bahamas. Volstead Act leads to prohibition in United States
1920	Bahamas included in Canada West Indies Trade Treaty
1921	Royal Mail service from Britain to Bahamas begins
1925	Government High School opened
1929	Hurricane
	Pan American daily flights to Miami
1931	Census of population 60,000
1933	Prohibition ended in United States
	Inter island charter air services begun
1935	First Labour union formed
1934–43	Sir Harry Oakes develops the Bahamas
1936	Bahamas Airways formed
	Broadcasting station opened
	Labour minimum wage act
1938	Exports valued at £182,000
1939	Collapse of sponge industry
1940–45	Duke of Windsor Governor of the Bahamas
1940	Americans begin construction of seaplane base at George Town Exuma
1942	Wage riots

1943	New Providence air fields completed
1945–60	The Retreat from Empire
1949	Hotels Encouragement Act. 32,018 tourists
1950	Commercial broadcasting began in Nassau
1953	Formation of Progressive Liberal Party
1955	Grand Bahamas Port Authority Act
1956	Dupuch Bill against racial discrimination
1957	General strike on New Providence
	Bahamas Federation of Labour formed
1958	United Bahamian party formed
	Taxi Drivers strike
1959	Huntington Hartford begins development of Paradise Island
1960	Abraham's Bay devastated by hurricane. Harold Macmillan's 'Wind of Change' speech in Capetown. PLP win by-elections. Amendment to 1955 Act (Hawksbill Creek Agreement)
1962	Women vote for first time
1964	Ministry of Tourism formed
	Internal self government under new constitution
1965	Companies Registration Act
	Submarine testing base established on Tongue of Ocean
1966	Bahamas use decimal coinage equivalent US dollar
	Second amendment to Hawksbill Creek Act
1968	Education Act. Compulsory and free between 5 and 12
	Over 1 million tourists
1969	Advanced Constitution effective in May. Cabinet government instituted
1971	Bahamas Development Corporation established
	Free National Movement formed
1972	Direct dialling by cable between Nassau, Freeport, West Palm Beach (233 miles)

Green Paper estimates a population of 250,000 by 1980

18 June 1973	Bahamasair formed
10 July 1973	Bahamas Independence Day

LIGHTHOUSES ERECTED

1859	Great Isaacs
1860	Cay Lobos
1863	Stirrup's Cay, Elbow Cay
1868	Cattle Island, Inagua
1876	Bird Rock

Bibliography

The Overseas Development Administration's Land Resources Division of Tolworth Tower Surbiton published in 1971 a 74-page booklet which contains a useful up to date list of publications dealing with the Bahamas under the headings of Agriculture, Animal Science, Botany, Climatology, Crops, Cultural Studies, Economics, Forestry, Geoscience, Land Tenure, Maps, Miscellaneous Natural Resources, Population, Soil Science and Water Resources. The wide-ranging modern specialist interest in the Bahamas is revealed in this list.

For the ordinary reader the best single introduction is still to be found in *The Bahama Islands* edited by George Burbank Shattuck of John Hopkins University for the Geographical Society of Baltimore in 1905. It is a large volume and deals comprehensively with a diversity of Bahamian topics of major importance.

The most concise modern history of the Bahamas is by Michael Craton. It was first published in 1962 in London and has since been reprinted. Interesting sidelights on the development of communications to and in the islands are given in *The Postage Stamps and Postal History of the Bahamas*, which was published in London in 1950.

Colourful pictures of the islands are vividly shown in Hans W. Hannau's large volume *The Bahama Islands in Full Colour* and in a pocket edition by the same author of *Islands of the Bahamas* in full colour.

The Bahamas Handbook and Businessman's Annual is a topical yearly presentation of the islands published by Etienne Dupuch Jnr of Nassau.

Useful general information is contained in the *Diver's Guide to all the Bahamas* published in Melbourne, Florida.

The most authoritative guide to the islands and one recognised as an official publication of the Ministry of Tourism is the *Yachtsman's Guide to the Bahamas* published yearly by Tropical Isle

Publishers of Coral Gables Florida. It is essential equipment for anyone thinking of cruising in the islands, and a mine of information for the general reader. It is liberally strewn with maps.

Neuroses in the Sun, by a Bahamian Doctor Timothy O. McCartney, will help the understanding of persons who seek to probe beneath the surface of today's Bahamas. It was published in Nassau in 1971.

Also published in Nassau in 1972 is *The Quiet Revolution in the Bahamas*, by Senator Doris L. Johnson. This book traces the events which brought to power the political party which led the islands into independence.

The Innocent Isle, by Zoe C. Durrell (1972) gives a settler's view of Great Abaco and contains interesting line drawings of plants, birds and shells.

Bush Medicine in the Bahamas is a slim volume containing 60 illustrations of plants, shrubs and vines which are still widely used by Bahamians. It is published by a Bahamian journalist, Mrs. Leslie Higgs, who owns the copyright.

Fascinating illustrations and tales of the Bahamas are preserved in four chapters of Lady Brassey's *In the Trades, the Tropics and the Roaring Forties* (London, 1885).

Three years later L. D. Powles recorded his vivid experiences of the islands in *The Land of the Pink Pearl* (London), a book which even then foresaw that new winds of change would blow through the shuttered jalousies of political power.

J. H. Stark, in *The History and Guide to the Bahamas* (1891) was more appreciative of Nassau, which was already then becoming popular with visitors from the United States. His illustrations assist the reader to realise how solid Nassau had become for a prosperous minority before the dawn of the twentieth century.

In 1949 two reprints were made of great value to the student of eighteenth century Nassau. One entitled *History of the Isle of Providence* (1949) was taken from Oldmixon's *History of the British Empire in America* (first issued in 1708 and revised in 1741). The other, *Bahamian Interlude* (1949) was taken from *Memories of P. H. Bruce* (1782).

Of especial political interest are Harcourt Malcolm's *Historical Documents relating to the Bahamas* (1910) and his *History of the House of Assembly*.

Johnson's *A General History of the Pirates*, edited by Arthur L. Hayward and reprinted in London, 1955, puts Bahamian pirates in the perspective of piracy as a profession.

One of the most popular books on the islands is *Out Island Doctor* (London, 1962) written by E. Cottman, whose green-painted castle on a hill is a landmark for pilots approaching Marsh Harbour's airport. A personal interpretation of the islands as they were in the earlier half of the twentieth century is given by Sir Etienne Dupuch in *Tribune Story*, which is hinged around the family newspaper still edited by his daughter.

Official attitudes to the islands during World War II are effectively presented in Professor Henry Richardson's *Review of Economic Conditions and Post-War Problems* (1944).

A more leisurely Bahamas is projected in G. J. H. Northcroft's *Sketches of Summerland in 1906*.

In marked contrast is *Inagua*, by Gilbert C. Klingel (London 1942). Few books on the islands derive from so active a communion between man and the encounters he makes with nature in several forms. Another remarkable book, centred on Andros, is Paul A. Zahl's *Flamingo Hunt* (1953).

Helpful for an appreciation of the historical background preceding settlement by the Lord Proprietors is A. P. Thornton's *West Indian Policy under the Restoration*.

An excellent modern biography of the First Earl of Shaftesbury, who was the most active of the Lords Proprietors, is by K. H. D. Haley. *The Andros Islanders*, by Keith F. Otterbein, (University of Kansas 1966) is a fascinating study of the people who put down roots on the largest island of the Bahamas.

The Third World Group Bahamas Independence issue shows the Bahamian people as they look to representatives of the new society in the making.

A mine of information which is useful for the traveller to the Bahamas, or anywhere overseas, is to be found in a 32-page free pamphlet prepared by *BOAC*. It is called *Before You Take off* and contains all the information you might otherwise discover too late.

Index